HEARST CASTLE

An Interpretive History of
W. R. Hearst's San Simeon Estate

by Nancy E. Loe

FOR MARTY
WHO SHOWED ME HOW THE GAME IS PLAYED

Published under license from Hearst San Simeon State Historical Monument.
"Hearst Castle," "Hearst Monument," "La Cuesta Encantada," and "The Enchanted Hill"
are trademarks and service marks of Hearst San Simeon State Historical Monument.

Produced by Companion Press
Santa Barbara, California
Jane Freeburg, Publisher/Editor

Designed by Lucy Brown
Cover photo handtinted by Peggy Lindt

Printed in Hong Kong by Dai Nippon Printing Company, Ltd.

ISBN 0-944197-27-2 (paper) ~ ISBN 0-944197-46-9 (cloth)
98 99 ~ 6   5   4   3

Illustration Credits

Academy of Motion Picture Arts & Sciences: 83, 88 left. Bison Archives: 12 bottom. California Polytechnic State University, Special Collections Department (Julia Morgan Collection): Front Cover, 1, 3, 5, 7, 8, 9, 10–11, 12 top, 13, 14, 16–17, 18–19, 20, 21, 22 top, 24, 25 top, 26, 27 right, 28–29, 30 bottom, 32, 33 left and center right, 34, 35, 36, 37 bottom, 41, 44–45, 48, 49, 50 bottom, 64, 65 top right, 67 left, 68 right, 75, 76, 77, 78 top, 81, 82 right, 92 left, 93 bottom right. Hearst Monument Archives: 15 left, 22 bottom, 27 left, 30 top, 31, 37 top, 39, 54 right, 55, 56 top right, 57 lower left and lower right, 58 left, 65 left, 65 right center, 67 right, 71, 72 left, 78 center, 79, 80, 84, 87 lower right, 88 right, 90, back flap bottom. Hearst Monument (Doug Allen) front flap bottom, 57 top, 60, 61 top right, (Zdravko Barov) 51 center, (John Blades) 1, 2, 25 bottom, 33 top right, 38, 40 left, 43, 50 top, 51 top, 52–53, 54 center left, 56 top left and lower right, 61 right center and bottom, 62 left, 72 right, 82 left, 84 left, 87 top, 95, back flap top, back cover (Ellis Sawyer) 66, 74, 93 top, 94, (Robert Latson) 59 right, (Ken Raveill) 58 right, 59 left, 62 right, 63, 73, 91, 92, (Julie Reitern) 89, (Gene Russell) 54 top left, (Amber Wisdom) Front flap top, 4, 40 right, 46, 47, 68 left, 70, 85, 86. © Time Warner, Inc., used by permission: 15 top right, Larry Ulrich: 6.

A detail of the marble statue The Three Graces, above, which stands in the garden opposite La Casa del Mar.

Julia Morgan's sketch for a ceiling panel in the main library of La Casa Grande, opposite, demonstrates her ability to incorporate architectural pieces from W. R. Hearst's vast art collections into her designs.

CONTENTS

CHAPTER ONE

A Remarkable Partnership:
Julia Morgan & W. R. Hearst   7

CHAPTER TWO

Commanding the Coast:
San Simeon Takes Shape   21

CHAPTER THREE

Gathering His Greatest Pleasures:
Art & Architecture   47

CHAPTER FOUR

A Glamorous & Exciting Weekend:
Guests at San Simeon   77

CHAPTER ONE

A Remarkable Partnership: Julia Morgan & W. R. Hearst

S an Simeon, the storied California estate of publisher William Randolph Hearst, enjoys a commanding view of the Pacific Ocean from a crest of the Santa Lucia mountains. Popularly known as either Hearst Castle or San Simeon, the estate is now a state historical monument that has attracted twenty-five million visitors since it opened to the public in 1958. The product of more than two decades of intense collaboration between Hearst and architect Julia Morgan, Hearst Castle offers an intriguing blend of natural beauty, architecture, art, and history.

Hearst and Morgan shared many of the traits necessary to this uncommon endeavor: keen minds, legendary stamina, encyclopedic recall, a love of arts and antiquities, and, perhaps above all, an innate feel for the California setting that inspired their work. Much has been made of Hearst's "dream" in creating San Simeon, and of the romantic name (*La Cuesta Encantada* or The Enchanted Hill) he used to christen it. But had he or Morgan been merely dreamers, the Santa Lucia hills would still graze cattle undisturbed and a remarkable partnership would never have been formed.

A complex man born to great wealth, William Randolph Hearst could have led a life of leisure, yet he vigorously managed a publishing and media empire for sixty-five of his eighty-eight years. He is commonly remembered for fomenting war against Spain at the turn of the twentieth century, yet he opposed American entry into world war in 1914 and again in 1939. His publications extolled the virtues of American family life, yet he was estranged from his wife for most of their marriage. Despite the scope of his influence, those who knew Hearst personally recall his quiet presence.

La Cuesta Encantada
For a time the Hearst estate at San Simeon, opposite, was referred to as "Las Estrellas," a name chosen by W. R. Hearst's wife, Millicent. In 1924 the publisher substituted "The Enchanted Hill" after discovering their first choice was already in use at a neighboring ranch. Hearst continued his father's practice of buying land until he had accumulated nearly 250,000 acres of central California real estate and fifty miles of coastline. The decorative detail sketch for a frieze, above, and a pastel rendering for a tile border, above left, are two of many thousands of sketches architect Julia Morgan and her staff made for San Simeon.

Julia Morgan's earliest sketches for San Simeon featured a single tower that, in her words, "shows the 'Ronda' motif for the main building."

An intensely private woman, Julia Morgan possessed drive and determination equal in measure to Hearst's. Her distinguished career as an architect made her a pioneer in her field and in women's history. In the opinion of San Francisco architectural critic Allan Temko, "This great Californian . . . deserves in American architecture at least as high a place as Mary Cassatt in American painting, or Edith Wharton in American letters." Another writer, Elinor Richey, rendered the gender distinction unnecessary: Morgan's work is "outstanding not only for its thoroughness, diversity, and volume . . . but also for its stylistic innovation and influence."

In April of 1919, shortly before he inherited his family's fortune, William Randolph Hearst and Julia Morgan met in her San Francisco office to begin the design and planning of an extraordinary estate filled with European art. The four Mediterranean-influenced residences would be the destination of many famous guests throughout the 1920s and 1930s.

The land near San Simeon Bay was acquired beginning in 1865 by Hearst's father, George, a rough-hewn Missouri-born man who wrested fortunes from the Comstock, Homestake, Ontario, and Anaconda mines. George's shrewd abilities in mining and real estate established the family fortune, which doubled and redoubled under his guidance. Among his first real estate purchases were the original Mexican ranchos of *Piedras Blancas, San Simeón,* and *Santa Rosa,* portions of which were bought for as little as seventy cents an acre. George Hearst confined his construction at the ranch to a wharf, a relatively modest Italianate two-story house, and the outbuildings necessary to raise cattle and horses. Eventually he added a racetrack as his interest in horse breeding and racing grew.

Concerned about his son's spend-thrift attitude toward money, George Hearst left his entire estate to his wife,

Phoebe, upon his death in 1891. Phoebe Hearst generously (if sometimes grudgingly) bankrolled her son's publishing ventures, art collections, and (in her words) "mania for travel," until her own death in the influenza epidemic of 1919.

With the resources of the Hearst fortune finally at hand, W. R. told Morgan he was "tired of going up there and camping in tents" and wanted "something that would be more comfortable" at San Simeon. Morgan employee Walter Steilberg recalled Hearst showing Morgan a series of books on bungalows that the publisher had found "prowling around second-hand book stores." The books sparked his desire for something "simple" 1,600 feet above sea level on "Camp Hill." The location of his family's tent city during summers past, the site had sentimental value for Hearst, but presented a series of daunting challenges for his architect. William Randolph Hearst, Jr., the publisher's second son, recalled:

> The experts told Pop that it couldn't be done. No one could build an adequate foundation for a large home up there on the crest of that steep hill overlooking the Pacific and the little village of San Simeon. There was no proper building material available—no lumber, no nearby steel or iron. Even if such materials were [there], a rising, curving road would have to be constructed out of the wilderness. And it was more than a five-mile pull . . . to the mountaintop. . . . It was a crazy idea. The experts told the old man to forget it.

But Morgan *was* an expert, and she committed herself to the project with as much enthusiasm as Hearst himself. After she personally walked the site in August, Morgan proceeded rapidly: plotting the arrangement of three "bungalows" and a large central structure, hiring a construction manager, reinforcing George Hearst's forty-three-year-old wharf, ordering the first construction materials, and grading the path that cattle and horses had worn up the hillside. Remarkably, in mid-September of 1919, a mere five weeks after Morgan first visited the site, she told Hearst construction was ready to commence. He replied:

> *My dear Miss Morgan: I have just sent you a telegram saying that we are ready to go ahead with the main building. . . . I am having the road bettered but we will have difficulty in getting heavy things up the hill in slippery weather. We should get them up <u>now</u>. . . . I want to concentrate on the main building and <u>get it done</u>. You will find a lot of motifs at the Hacienda [del Pozo de Verona, the late Phoebe Hearst's country estate] in the stuff belonging to me. Some of them have been there for a long time—columns &c. Others I have sent lately. . . . I will send more from the East, but you will not need these things much until we come to interior decoration.*

On November 21, 1919, Morgan wrote to Hearst in New York:

> *The "Cleone," a very disreputable old coaster, sailed yesterday afternoon from the Oakland side for San Simeon, fully insured, with cement, lumber for forms, nails, reinforcing bars for concrete, ready roofing and a second hand band saw and rock crusher. It should reach your wharf on Sunday, and Mr. Lee [the ranch manager] will have the ranch men help [construction superintendent Herbert] Washburn's men unload. The trucks are not standing up very well, so it may be a couple of weeks before it reaches the mountain top.*

Morgan's forecast was correct: it took four days to sail the supplies in from Oakland and two weeks before most of the steamer's cargo had been hauled up to the construction site using a combination of chain-driven trucks and horse teams. Morgan had faced a waterfront strike in Oakland, insurance troubles, delivery delays, lingering wartime supply shortages, winter rains, and design changes by her client, but the battle had been joined: construction had finally begun on Hearst's seaside complex.

As Hearst travelled frequently between coasts and in Europe and Morgan maintained her practice in San Francisco, many of their ideas and decisions were committed to paper, documenting the complex and detailed process of bringing San Simeon to life. Morgan's letters are as businesslike as the reputation that now precedes her, but the business is often dispatched with keen diplomacy and a dry wit. Her greatest challenge working with Hearst undoubtedly was his compulsive need to change work that was either in progress or already finished. Even Hearst acknowledged this trait. In March of 1920 he wired Morgan:

> ALL THE LITTLE HOUSES ARE STUN-
> NING AND THE SLIGHTLY DIFFERENT
> TREATMENT MAKES THEM VERY
> ATTRACTIVE . . . PLEASE COMPLETE
> THEM BEFORE I CAN THINK UP ANY
> MORE CHANGES

Getting the funds from Hearst to settle accounts and meet payrolls was Morgan's greatest non-architectural difficulty. Large amounts of Morgan's time were taken trying to reconcile Hearst's unrestrained enthusiasm for building and art collecting with his chronic lack of ready cash. "Mr. Hearst has the habit of ignoring his obligations," one art dealer plaintively, if delicately, wrote to Morgan. Hearst's own directives reveal a mercurial approach: letters demanding contruction be shut down entirely were countermanded by tele-grams requesting rush jobs before the imminent appearance of guests.

Early in the project Morgan approached Hearst directly regarding her architectural fees. "If satisfactory to

Crews poured concrete continuously from August of 1922 to the spring of 1924 just to complete the two stories of the main building as originally designed. Even in the midst of construction, Hearst directed that landscaping and tree-planting begin.

This view of "Camp Hill" dates from the early 1920s, showing construction in progress on the main building. La Casa del Sol, nearing completion, is at right.

you, may I suggest that payment for my work be made on this plan: Instead of paying the usual 3½% when the work is begun, and 2½% as it progresses, that your office pay me $500.00 on account on the first of each month until an amount equal to the commission shall have been paid. I have been using this method and have found it satisfactory both to my clients and myself." Hearst readily agreed to the plan, but in the next three years seldom lived up to it. Later Morgan requested that Hearst deposit $25,000 in the San Simeon account each month, from which Morgan would "run the job," as she put it. Hearst again agreed, but seldom complied.

Given Hearst's zeal for building and art collecting, the idea of "bungalows" or "cottages" rapidly dissolved into protean plans for the unfinished, yet formidable estate that stands today. Over the years, three guest houses and a main building were built and linked by an esplanade and a series of garden terraces. Also added were indoor and outdoor swimming pools, a movie theater with a small stage, tennis courts, a billiard room, a wine cellar, two libraries, a private zoo, dog kennels, a thoroughbred horse ranch and miles of bridle paths, a pergola, and a landing strip and airplane hangar. No matter how large his estate grew over the succeeding years, Hearst usually referred to the place simply as "the ranch."

Less glamorous but necessary to the daily operation of San Simeon were a reservoir, poultry ranch, dairy, vegetable garden, orchards, greenhouses, hothouse, kitchen (with larder and pantries), powerhouse, telephone office (with switchboard, shortwave radio, teletype and telegraph), ten-car garage, fire truck, warehouses, a small village of houses for key staff members, a dining room and sleeping quarters for domestic help, a bunkhouse for cowboys, cowboy camps, and a cattle ranch with miles of dirt roads.

Equally important were the many shops and skilled workers necessary to build and maintain the estate, including carpenters, electricians, plumbers, blacksmiths, plasterers, ironmongers, painters, and artisans—many from Europe—who worked with cast stone, iron, wood, glass, or tile. Large canvas tents were erected for housing and feeding the construction crew; wooden barracks and a mess hall later replaced some of these tents.

Morgan's rigorous training in classical architecture at the *École des Beaux-Arts*, as well as her considerable experience working with reinforced concrete, equipped her well for the complex process before her. Several writers have christened Morgan a "pioneer" in concrete construction, but in 1920 reinforced concrete was "not an unusual construction technique, but a successful building method practiced in California for at least thirty years," notes historian Robert Pavlik. Morgan had the talent necessary to work with all building materials, including stone, wood, and concrete. Pavlik writes that "Morgan was able to apply both her engineering and architectural training to the challenges of reinforced concrete construction, while at the same time learning from and studying the work of other contemporary architects who were also building with steel and cement."

Morgan supervised the rock blasting on the site of the main building's foundations, directing its future use in concrete produced with piped-in water and sand (that had been washed free of salt) from local beaches. Her use of reinforced concrete was also a practical choice, well suited to withstand fire and earthquake, two ever-present dangers haunting any construction in California.

Morgan's reputation for respecting the wishes of her clients and her diplomatic personality further ensured her success with the changeable and intense W. R. Hearst. The collaborative effort

Morgan staff member Dorothy Wormser Coblentz, above, burns packing crates in the village of San Simeon, where she worked cataloging Hearst's art purchases.

Below, Hearst and Morgan at work on the terrace at San Simeon.

Although La Casa Grande became the formal name for the largest structure on "Camp Hill," the edifice was usually called "main building" or "m.b." by Hearst and Morgan. At the bottom of Morgan's colored pencil sketch, opposite, Hearst has written his opinion of the design.

between Hearst and Morgan "shows Hearst at his most charming, a devout amateur in the best sense of the word," according to Morgan biographer Sara Holmes Boutelle. In their many years of correspondence, they addressed each other exclusively as "Miss Morgan" and "Mr. Hearst." While Hearst deferred to Morgan's judgment on innumerable occasions, he always used "we" when proposing new ideas. At the end of 1919 he wrote to Morgan, saying, "I wired you not to do . . . anything that you do not wholly approve of. I make a lot of suggestions and if any of them are impracticable or imperfect from an architectural point of view, please discard them and substitute whatever you think is better."

Much of Morgan's time that first autumn was devoted to philosophical discussions with Hearst about the architectural style and intent of the estate. After great deliberation and much consultation of their respective libraries of architectural books, Morgan and Hearst favored the blended style of Spanish Colonial architecture that characterized the 1915 Panama-Pacific International Exposition in San Francisco

and the Panama-California Exposition in San Diego, elaborations of the Mission Revival style popular in California for the previous twenty-five years. But Hearst was also quick to note that he "wished for something a little different from what other people are doing in California," which ultimately led to the unique mingling of styles and periods that is San Simeon. Robert Pavlik notes, "Hearst was both influenced by and influential in the movement to define and establish a sense of regional history and culture for California. His fondness for Mediterranean motifs and the Spanish style of architecture began with his early trips to Europe and were manifested as early as the construction of his mother's Pleasanton estate, a task in which he took great pleasure and personal interest."

Julia Morgan continued a full-time practice from her San Francisco office, devoting her weekends to on-site supervision at San Simeon. Later in the project, she confined herself to Monday visits on-site. Bjarne Dahl, once a young drafter in Morgan's firm, remembers, "All her life was work—morning, day, and night. I went down [to San Simeon] one

I think there should be ten feet more width between the towers for the central gabled building. I think this will help rather than hurt the front elevation and it will be much better inside for the big assembly room giving that 85 ft length, and clearing the tapestries from above the doors into the refectory.

When work started at San Simeon Julia Morgan was forty-seven and W. R. Hearst fifty-six. "There was no margin for error [working] for Miss Morgan. . . . No thing escaped her eyes," remembered tilesetter Joseph Giarritta. Of Hearst, construction superintendent Maurice McClure said, "He was a very difficult man to work for. He could not understand an error. He would fire a man on the spot for little or nothing. I do not know how I survived for ten years."

Julia Morgan was direct when dealing with employees, as Morgan biographer Virginia Wadsworth relates: "When a talented young drafter drew a staircase that was impossible to climb, she called him aside. 'Well, young man,' she said, because she never remembered names, 'I can't deal with fiction writers.' " With her clients, Morgan favored a more diplomatic approach.

time with Miss Morgan and spent the day looking over things. She kept busy all day long. We took a train from San Francisco down there, and she worked all day long. Then, when we came back the next morning, I was tired and had to stay home. She went right to work again!"

Although Morgan hired young women and men into her firm, she sometimes grew disenchanted with them because they were not prepared to work as hard as she did. Architect Dorothy Wormser Coblentz worked for Morgan both in San Francisco and at San Simeon, but believed that Morgan "didn't realize that people had private lives" that made "eighteen hours [of work] a day" impossible.

Morgan's dedication to her profession was noted by family and friends as well as employees. She would become so engrossed in her work that one friend accused her of living at her office on nothing but Hershey bars and coffee. Dahl remembers, "When we would be working at night [in the San Francisco office], she'd have a soda cracker and chew on that with maybe a glass of water."

Virginia Wadsworth, another Morgan biographer, remarked on her close relationships with family members and how she looked forward to attending holiday gatherings, but "before they knew it, she would be thumbing through a book on architecture—or drawing ideas on a scrap of paper."

At the École des Beaux-Arts, Morgan had excelled at such opulent assignments as palace ballrooms and art galleries for imaginary clients. Twenty years later, projects of such scale and majesty again flowed from Morgan's pen and drafting table, taking shape on a California hilltop for the larger-than-life William Randolph Hearst.

William Randolph Hearst

Phoebe Apperson Hearst, top, endowed her son with her own love of art and travel. A formidable woman, Mrs. Hearst was a great philanthropist who underwrote many projects at the University of California at Berkeley.

W. R. Hearst on a visit to Germany, above, in the early 1930s.

Hearst appeared on the cover of rival magazine Time, *opposite, far right, in 1927.*

Opposite, Don Pancho Estrada, a descendent of the family who held the original Mexican land grants for San Simeon, rides with W. R. Hearst. Their friendship began in childhood; Estrada was one of the few who addressed Hearst as "Willie."

William Randolph Hearst was born on April 29, 1863, in San Francisco, the only child of George and Phoebe Apperson Hearst. His father was a self-made man, whose first fortune came from the silver mines of the Comstock Lode in 1859. Young Willie was considered precocious by his mother, who encouraged his early appreciation of the fine arts. As George Hearst became increasingly involved in his mining and real estate ventures, Phoebe Hearst devoted her attention and intellect to her son. She also turned her considerable energy to philanthrophy and art collecting. The Hearsts were in their element in early San Francisco, for George Hearst sought power as assiduously as Phoebe courted culture. Their son would inherit their determination and love of both worlds in equal measure.

The family's wealth allowed Willie Hearst and his mother to make two Grand Tours of Europe by the time he was sixteen. Hearst's fondness for art collecting began at age ten, and came to be a compelling and ultimately indispensable part of his adult life.

In 1882 Will enrolled at Harvard College, where he successfully managed the college's humor magazine and displayed great interest in entertainment and the theater. During the 1884 presidential elections, he wrote to his father, now a U. S. senator, that he had organized a campus political group "which includes all the democratic dudes in college, and, for a fact, most of the swells are for [Democratic candidate Grover] Cleveland." Unfortunately, young Will did not devote as much time to his formal studies as he did to the Harvard *Lampoon* and the Hasty Pudding Club and was asked to leave in his junior year.

As Will's interest in the theater, politics, and art collecting grew, his ability to live within his allowance did not. His letters to his mother are a virtual catalog of funds spent, followed by pleas for additional sums. He also wrote to his father that he was considering a future career in "law, politics or journalism, and under favorable circumstances it might be possible to combine all three."

At twenty-three Hearst plunged into journalism as editor and publisher of the foundering San Francisco *Examiner,* a Democratic newspaper his father owned. He successfully applied his own enormous energy, his family's substantial financial backing, and the sensational news techniques of New York publisher Joseph Pulitzer to the *Examiner.* Hearst went on to purchase or begin papers in New York, Chicago, Seattle, Los Angeles, Boston, and twenty other American cities. He further enlarged his publishing empire by buying or founding such magazines as *Motor, Connoisseur, Good Housekeeping, Cosmopolitan,* and *Popular Mechanics.*

Hearst married Millicent Willson, a New York entertainer, on the eve of his fortieth birthday. They had five sons: George; William Randolph, Jr.; John; and twin boys, Randolph and David. The family lived primarily in New York, but made frequent, if elaborate, camping trips to the family ranch at San Simeon in central California.

The presidential elections of 1900 rekindled Hearst's interest in political office, and he won a seat in the House of Representatives in 1902. He would win re-election two years later from the same West Side district of New York City, but before he began his second term, Hearst ran for mayor of New York City. Both contemporary observers and political historians believe Hearst won, but the crooked Tammany political machine in New York threw the election to their candidate. He next attempted and won the Democratic nomination in 1906 for governor of New York, but was again thwarted at the polls. Hearst would make attempts in 1908 and 1912 to win the presidency, but his efforts were doomed. He remained a powerful political figure, courted by candidates not only for public endorsement in print, but also for his private affirmation to party leaders.

In 1913 Hearst expanded his empire into the production of newsreels. By the early 1920s Hearst had formed Cosmopolitan Productions in New York City to make newsreels, serials, and feature films. In 1924 Hearst moved his studio

to California, where he, along with his companion, astress Marion Davies, and other stars under Cosmopolitan contract, forged an alliance the following year with movie mogul Louis B. Mayer at Metro-Goldwyn-Mayer.

Phoebe Apperson Hearst contracted influenza in the worldwide epidemic of 1919 and died in April, leaving the entire Hearst fortune, most of her art collections, and widespread real estate and business holdings to her only child. Once it was within his means to build at San Simeon, Hearst retained architect Julia Morgan to begin design and construction of the remarkable estate that hosted a wide circle of famous guests in the 1920s and 1930s.

By 1937 years of profligate spending, coinciding with the Great Depression, left Hearst and his media empire $126 million in debt. John Francis Neylan, a Hearst adviser, explained: "Money as such bores him. . . . He is a builder. He wants to build buildings, newspapers, magazines, hotels, ranches. His idea is to build, build, build all the time. . . . In his makeup there is just

a blank space in relation to money." The timely advice of lawyers and financiers, liquidation of some real estate, newspaper and art holdings, and increased newspaper sales during World War II rescued the Hearst Corporation.

As World War II ended, limited construction resumed at San Simeon under the direction of Morgan's protégé, Warren McClure. In 1948 heart problems forced Hearst to leave the estate permanently. He retreated to a relatively modest Beverly Hills house with Davies to be close to the specialists who maintained his faltering health.

On August 14, 1951, William Randolph Hearst died at the age of eighty-eight. His widow and five sons gathered in San Francisco for the funeral and the interment at Cypress Lawn Cemetery. His 125-page will is one of the longest ever filed in California. A portion of the estate, believed to total nearly $220 million, was left in trust to his family; the remainder was bequeathed to the Hearst Foundation as a charitable trust.

4'-9"

"RUNNING THE JOB" AT SAN SIMEON
Construction of San Simeon spanned more than two decades, during which architect Julia Morgan and client William Randolph Hearst consulted each other frequently by mail, cable, and telegram. Hearst's directives to Morgan—often several a day arrived at her offices in the Merchants Exchange Building in San Francisco—covered diverse topics from room dimensions to workers' wages to urgent requests to "get it done."

The drawing of the main building and its surrounding guest houses, center, records ideas and notations from both Hearst (at upper right) and Morgan (at lower right).

Morgan often used photographs of the hilltop site to make quick sketches of possible new buildings, like the concept for an animal shelter, below right.

A letter from architect to client, opposite, includes Hearst's comments and a rough drawing of a terrace with landscaping.

Morgan's thumbnail sketches fill all the available space on an advertising page from The Saturday Evening Post, *opposite, top.*

POSTAL TELEGRAPH – COMMERCIAL CABLES
RECEIVED AT MAIN OFFICE
POSTAL TELEGRAPH BUILDING
COR. MARKET & BATTERY STS.
SAN FRANCISCO
TELEPHONE: KEARNY 1000
CLARENCE H. MACKAY, PRESIDENT
TELEGRAM
DELIVERY NO.
This is a fast Day Telegram unless otherwise indicated by signal after the number of words:—"N.L." (Night Lettergram) or "Nite" (Night Telegram). 18—47097

C29CBJH 2INL   1233A 15
NEWYORK JAN 14
MISS JULIA MORGAN
1320 JAN 14 '20
ARTICHECT MERCHANTS EX BLDG SANFRANCISCO
WHAT IS CEILING HEIGHT IN COTTAGES I THINK IT SHOULD
BE NOT LESS THAN TEN FEET POSSIBLY TEN AND A
HALF
W R HEARST

POSTAL TELEGRAPH – COMMERCIAL CABLES
CLARENCE H. MACKAY, PRESIDENT
RECEIVED AT MAIN OFFICE
POSTAL TELEGRAPH BUILDING
COR. MARKET & BATTERY STS.
SAN FRANCISCO
TELEPHONE: KEARNY 1000
TELEGRAM
DELIVERY NO.
This is a fast Day Telegram unless otherwise indicated by signal after the number of words:—"N.L." (Night Lettergram) or "Nite" (Night Telegram). 18—47097

75cbgx 86 N.L.   340am8
JX.Newyork Mar.7,1920
86 MAR 8 '20

Miss Julia Morgan,
Architect Merchants Exg Blg San Francisco
Mr.Bogart promises the trucks within a week I have sent fairchild to ranch to construct the road.You have authority to employ workmen at what ever price necessary please let me know if the work is still sufficiently incomplete to allow of the lengthening of parlors and bedrooms in houses B.and C.in addition to the addition of the Loggias and porches as telegraphed if so I would like to do it as I think the rooms are too small for comfort and permanent occupancy
W.R.Hearst

16

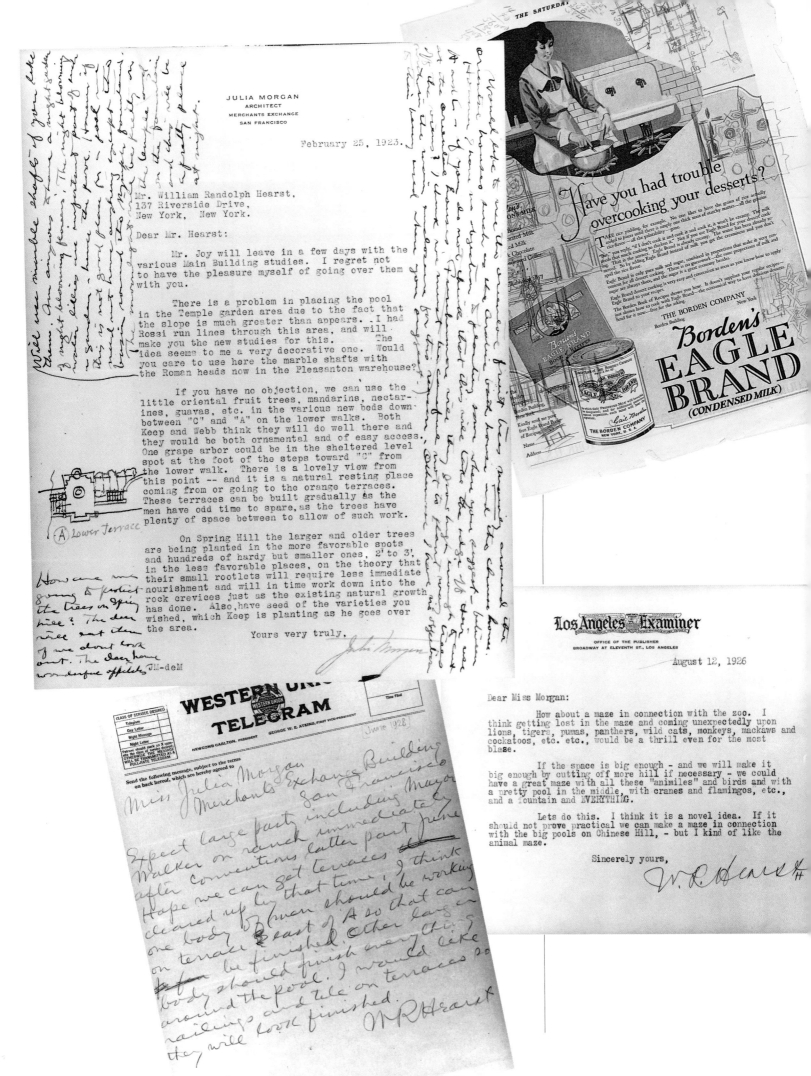

JULIA MORGAN
ARCHITECT
MERCHANTS EXCHANGE
SAN FRANCISCO

February 25, 1923.

Mr. William Randolph Hearst,
137 Riverside Drive,
New York, New York.

Dear Mr. Hearst:

Mr. Joy will leave in a few days with the
various Main Building studies. I regret not
to have the pleasure myself of going over them
with you.

There is a problem in placing the pool
in the Temple garden area due to the fact that
the slope is much greater than appears. I had
Rossi run lines through this area, and will
make you the new studies for this. The
idea seems to me a very decorative one. Would
you care to use here the marble shafts with
the Roman heads now in the Pleasanton warehouse?

If you have no objection, we can use the
little oriental fruit trees, mandarins, nectar-
ines, guavas, etc. in the various new beds down
between "C" and "A" on the lower walks. Both
Keep and Webb think they will do well there and
they would be both ornamental and of easy access.
One grape arbor could be in the sheltered level
spot at the foot of the steps toward "C" from
the lower walk. There is a lovely view from
this point -- and it is a natural resting place
coming from or going to the orange terraces.
These terraces can be built gradually as the
men have odd time to spare, as the trees have
plenty of space between to allow of such work.

On Spring Hill the larger and older trees
are being planted in the more favorable spots
and hundreds of hardy but smaller ones, 2' to 3',
in the less favorable places, on the theory that
their small rootlets will require less immediate
nourishment and will in time work down into the
rock crevices just as the existing natural growth
has done. Also, have seed of the varieties you
wished, which Keep is planting as he goes over
the area.

Yours very truly,

Julia Morgan

JM-deM

(A) Lower Terrace

How are we
going to protect
the trees on Spring
Hill? The deer
will eat them
if we don't look
out. The deer home
wonderful effects.

Will use number shafts if you like
them. Am anxious to see a night scene.
I ought becoming famous. The night becoming
water lilies are important parts of it.
Somehow I have the pure feeling
this is not good form. We must not
mind out how everything we plant will
begin new do anything with it.

While the center is in-
tended to be see
and partly pave
as present.

Los Angeles Examiner
OFFICE OF THE PUBLISHER
BROADWAY AT ELEVENTH ST., LOS ANGELES

August 12, 1926

Dear Miss Morgan:

How about a maze in connection with the zoo. I
think getting lost in the maze and coming unexpectedly upon
lions, tigers, pumas, panthers, wild cats, monkeys, mackaws and
cockatoos, etc. etc., would be a thrill even for the most
blase.

If the space is big enough - and we will make it
big enough by cutting off more hill if necessary - we could
have a great maze with all these "animiles" and birds and with
a pretty pool in the middle, with cranes and flamingos, etc.,
and a fountain and EVERYTHING.

Lets do this. I think it is a novel idea. If it
should not prove practical we can make a maze in connection
with the big pools on Chinese Hill, - but I kind of like the
animal maze.

Sincerely yours,

W. R. Hearst

WESTERN UNION
TELEGRAM

CLASS OF SERVICE DESIRED
Telegram
Day Letter
Night Message
Night Letter

NEWCOMB CARLTON, PRESIDENT   GEORGE W. E. ATKINS, FIRST VICE-PRESIDENT

[June 1928]

Send the following message, subject to the terms
on back hereof, which are hereby agreed to

Miss Julia Morgan
Merchants Exchange Building
San Francisco

Expect large party including
Walker on ranch immediately
after conventions latter part June
Hope we can get terraces
cleared up by that time. I think
one body of men should be working
on terrace east of A so that can
be finished. Other large
body should finish everything
around the pool. I would like
railings and tile on terraces so
they will look finished.

W R Hearst

17

Julia
Morgan,
Architect

Julia Morgan was born in San Francisco on January 20, 1872, the second child of five born to Charles Bill and Eliza Parmelee Morgan. She grew up in Oakland, California, where she was actively encouraged by her mother to excel as a scholar. As she began college, she briefly contemplated a career in medicine, but her interest in architecture was kindled by her mother's cousin, Pierre LeBrun, who designed the Metropolitan Life Insurance Tower, an early New York City skyscraper.

At this time only a handful of women were active in the profession, and few architecture programs accepted women. Morgan chose civil engineering as the closest equivalent and in the fall of 1890 entered the University of California at Berkeley, seven miles from her home, as one of just twenty women students in the entire student body—and the only woman enrolled in the School of Engineering. She was required to be chaperoned by her younger brother, Avery, while traveling to and from campus and in class. During her senior year at Berkeley, a technical drawing class provided her with a mentor, Bernard Maybeck, who encouraged Morgan to attend his Parisian alma mater, the *École Nationale et Spéciale des Beaux-Arts.*

In 1894 Julia Morgan earned her undergraduate degree in civil engineering and immediately began a year of work and private study with Maybeck, preparing for a *Beaux-Arts* education. Maybeck had apprised Morgan of the French system: students were accepted into an *atelier,* or studio, of a *Beaux-Arts*-trained architect, and sat for the highly competitive entrance exams. Students then were assigned a succession of *programmes,* or problems. The curriculum was renowned for the scope and majesty of

its assignments: a suite of rooms in a grand apartment of a palace, art galleries, opera houses, and other opulent environments fit for lavish, if imaginary, clients.

Morgan, now twenty-four, arrived in Paris and secured a place in the *atelier* of Marcel Perouse de Monclos. She prepared for the grueling entrance examinations, which presented the additional challenges of the French language and the metric system. Two unsuccessful attempts discouraged Morgan, until she learned that she had been failed deliberately by faculty members who, in the words of M. de Monclos, "did not wish to encourage young girls." Morgan was relieved that her work was not at fault and wrote home to say, "I'll try again next time anyway even without any expectations, just to show *'des jeunes filles'* are not discouraged."

Late in 1898, after two years of effort, Morgan was finally admitted to the school. She won honors for her work in mathematics, architecture, and design and advanced to the senior class in less than half the average time. In 1902 Julia Morgan became the first woman to receive *Beaux-Arts* certification in architecture. With her *diplôme* in hand, Morgan returned to Oakland that year and found work with architect John Galen Howard, who had won (by default) the competition underwritten by Phoebe Apperson Hearst to design a master building plan for the University of California. Howard boasted of Morgan as "the best and most talented designer, whom I have to pay almost nothing, as it [*sic*] is a woman."

In 1904 Morgan opened her own office in San Francisco, securing many residential commissions using a California vernacular style with distinct Arts and Crafts attributes, including exposed support beams, horizontal lines that blended into the landscape, and extensive use of shingles, California redwood, and earth tones.

Major institutional commissions, including rebuilding the Fairmont Hotel after the great San Francisco earthquake, called upon her experience with reinforced concrete and her training in engineering. Morgans biographer Sara Holmes Boutelle

Morgan's student identification card, top, from the École des Beaux-Arts, *taken in 1898. An accomplished artist as well as designer, Morgan created hundreds of colored pencil sketches and watercolors, above, during her years of study in Paris. She was awarded medals, right, signifying a first- or second-place finish, for four competitions entered while a Beaux-Arts student.*

notes that "approximately half of her clients were women and institutions for women. . . . Most of her important clients developed not as a result of accounts of her work in popular and professional journals, but from social connections and recommendations from former clients and a network of both women of wealth and women professionals of more modest economic means."

In 1902 Bernard Maybeck and Julia Morgan were retained by Phoebe Hearst to build at Wyntoon, Phoebe's northern California retreat. The next year Morgan was also hired to complete Phoebe's principal residence near Pleasanton, California. Phoebe Hearst and Grace Merriam Fisher, a Berkeley sorority sister of Morgan's, were influential in their recommendation of Morgan as architect for the Oakland YWCA (Young Women's Christian Association) in 1912. Morgan went on to design forty-one YWCA buildings in fifteen cities in California, Utah, and Hawaii. Morgan was also commissioned by Phoebe Hearst to work on one of Phoebe's last philanthropic gestures, the California seaside YWCA conference center called Asilomar, at Pacific Grove, for which Morgan designed thirteen structures between 1915 and 1920.

Phoebe Hearst's son, publisher William Randolph Hearst, first retained Morgan in 1910 for a residence in Santa Monica, but it was never built. She did construct a clapboard house for Hearst at his Grand Canyon property in 1914, and then designed the jewel-like Los Angeles *Examiner* building for Hearst the next year. Their longest collaboration, however, was on two of Hearst's estates, San Simeon in central California, beginning in 1919, and Wyntoon, near the California-Oregon border, beginning in 1930. Their greatest unrealized plans were to recreate the Santa Maria de Ovila monastery Hearst had had dismantled and shipped from Spain as a wing of the de Young Museum in San Francisco.

Morgan remained active professionally through the 1940s, touring abroad to gather new ideas. In 1951, the year Hearst died, she closed her San Francisco office

and retired. After several years of poor health, Morgan died in San Francisco in 1957 at the age of eighty-five.

Immersed in her work for over fifty years, Julia Morgan designed and built more than 700 structures, yet she never published any of her designs, declined interviews, and accepted but one honorary degree. In marked contrast to William Randolph Hearst, her most famous client, Morgan was a woman of few public words, insisting that her buildings speak for themselves.

Usually camera-shy, Julia Morgan poses, above, with Marianne—the baby elephant in Hearst's private zoo—in 1930. A portrait of the architect in 1926, left, shows Morgan at the midpoint of her successful and prolific career. One of many honors and commendations Morgan received during her career, the certificate of recognition, above, was presented to her in 1940 by the Women's Board of the Pageant of the Pacific, Golden Gate International Exposition.

CHAPTER TWO

Commanding the Coast: San Simeon Takes Shape

J ulia Morgan's obsessive dedication to her profession benefitted W. R. Hearst, who also was well-acquainted with eighteen-hour days crammed with details and decisions. Telegraph wires to San Francisco crackled with Hearst's resolutions, retractions, and revisions about San Simeon. Using hand-charted topographical maps of the rocky bluffs of "Camp Hill," Morgan painstakingly plotted and replotted the location of the main building (*La Casa Grande*) and its three surrounding guest houses, maneuvering around three of her client's objectives: superb views, undisturbed native oaks, and sufficient space for a large main terrace and walkways between the four buildings. In late 1919 Hearst, regarding one set of changes, wrote:

Dear Miss Morgan: I have no objection at all to the houses being moved farther down the hill. . . . We refer to them as little houses, but they are really not little houses. They are only little as compared to the big central building. They will cover a great deal of ground and shut out a good deal of the view. I think they should be dropped well down the hill and you need not hesitate to do this.

A few weeks after writing to Morgan urging her "to concentrate on the main building and get it done," he changed course and decided to begin construction on the three guest "cottages." Eager to occupy the buildings from the moment the first spadeful of earth was turned, Hearst hoped that the smaller structures could be completed more rapidly. The earliest construction efforts were turned to *La Casa del Mar*, or "A" House, which Hearst and his family would occupy, and its two companions, *La Casa del Monte* and *La Casa del Sol* ("B" and "C" Houses, respectively). Throughout the project, Hearst longed for two more guest houses, proposing English Tudor and Chinese styles. Morgan

LA CASA DEL SOL
Julia Morgan's watercolor sketch, opposite, of the third guest house built at San Simeon, La Casa del Sol. Hearst named the building for its view to the west, ideal for watching the sunset over the Pacific. Morgan also made a color sketch of the tile design used on the guest house's sitting room floor, above left.

Smoke from a distant brushfire hovers over this view of the quarters for San Simeon construction workers, top.

Above, Thaddeus Joy (at left) and Frank Humrich pose at the construction camp in the late 1920s. Joy was a valued Morgan employee who worked on-site at San Simeon for nearly ten years. Humrich, gilder imported from New York, assisted with the reproduction of antique wooden ceilings.

drew preliminary elevations for a Mediterranean-styled "D" House, but the number of guest houses remained at three.

Always particular about detail, Hearst lavished attention on La Casa del Mar, the largest and most elaborate of the structures that were still, at this point, referred to as "cottages" by Morgan and Hearst. The first building to be occupied on the hilltop, La Casa del Mar overlooks the Pacific and has eighteen rooms on three levels, totaling nearly 6,400 square feet of living space. La Casa del Monte, featuring northern mountain views, is the smallest of the three guest houses, with ten rooms and about 2,300 square feet of space. La Casa del Sol, built above a huge terrace positioned for guests to enjoy sunset ocean views, has eighteen rooms on three levels, covering approximately 3,100 square feet.

Morgan realized very early in the project that she needed both her own representative and a construction superintendent on-site who could follow her orders, maintain a stable work force, and make accurate and timely progress reports. Thaddeus Joy, a drafter whose name was on Morgan's office door, worked as her principal designer at San Simeon and in San Francisco for nearly a decade, until he became too ill to work in the late 1920s. He was succeeded by Warren McClure, who came to California from Michigan hoping to design period architecture for movie sets. McClure would remain at San Simeon until 1948.

During the many years of building at San Simeon, four men supervised construction workers: Herbert Washburn (1919-1922), Camille C. Rossi (1922-1932), George C. Loorz (1932-1940), and Maurice McClure (1945-1948). Each construction superintendent and his labor bosses designated "gangs" of workers for long-term projects, such as roads, fences, orchards, gardens, construction, cement, and pools.

Her first selection, Herbert Washburn, a young builder from

Monterey, was in Morgan's words, "much pleased at being chosen for the work and I think will make good." Long-time Morgan employee Walter Steilberg remembered Washburn "was a very quiet and amazingly efficient man who took care of all the complicated inspections and, I think, was as responsible as anyone for it [San Simeon] getting off to a proper start."

Washburn's first two assignments were improving the road to the hilltop and erecting a camp for the construction crew. Poor roads and the remote location meant that virtually all construction laborers and skilled workers lived on the site, first in tents and later in crude barracks. Some construction workers were not enthusiastic about staying for long, particularly during rainy winters. Morgan usually hired skilled workers she knew from the San Francisco Bay area, but laborers were often recruited locally.

The number of workers on the hilltop varied according to the season and Hearst's cash flow. In 1928 Morgan wrote to Hearst: "The full complement of men (75), plus the additional twenty men you authorized, are at work on the Hill," where they earned between two and four dollars a day, with one dollar held back for meals and lodging. Skilled workers, such as carpenters and plasterers, were paid union scale wages, minus a dollar a day for room and board.

David Christian, the camp's "bull cook" during the mid-1930s, reflected on his time at San Simeon: "I took care of the construction camp, ran the dining hall, and made sure everybody was charged a dollar a day for their meals. We had sometimes as many as a whole hundred at one time in there." Christian made daily trips to the village of San Simeon, where he picked up the mail, food, and other supplies that had arrived by steamer for the construction camp.

Hearst was mindful of the primitive living conditions for hilltop workers, reminding Morgan in September of

1929, "Please give the men the best food and the best cook you can possibly get. We do not have very luxurious quarters for them and we ought to have a very good kitchen."

In June of 1929 Hayes Perkins, a Scot who made tart observations in his diary during his eight years at Wyntoon and San Simeon, wrote: "The food supplied at the cookhouse is of excellent quality, but the manner of preparing it is atrocious. No kitchen help is hired other than Chinese. . . . Fats of every sort, whether beef, mutton, or pork or even vegetable go into one collective pot and are used in cooking steaks or anything else grease is used for. This gives many of us indigestion, and my stomach is in agonies of pain most of the time."

Hearst had difficulty understanding the dilemma Morgan faced recruiting and retaining construction workers, most of whom were used to the sights and sounds of cities. Morgan became responsible for occupying the crew on their off-hours, after Hearst learned of construction workers poaching wildlife on the ranch. In a temper, Hearst wrote to Morgan explicitly forbidding members of the crew to "wander over the ranch or to fish or to hunt. . . . They shall confine themselves to their legitimate business on the property. If you hired a plumber to fix your bathroom you would not expect him to be wandering around your parlor or reading your books in the library. . . ."

One solution Morgan chose was movies, a favorite diversion of Hearst himself. After improvising a sheet for a screen at the impromptu open-air theater, she reported to Hearst, "I have tried a moving picture show once a week which has been well worth the money in keeping down 'turn-over'. The operator brings his own machine, pays his expenses and shows seven reels for $30." Eventually she would add, in the words of Hayes Perkins, "a club house . . . where there are pool and billiard tables and

where the men may beef [complain] and smoke." The room was padlocked at 11 PM to preclude gambling and late hours.

During Washburn's tenure, the structural elements of the three guest houses were completed, as well as some interior work on La Casa del Mar and La Casa del Monte. Although popular among the workers, Washburn was dismissed in October of 1922 after nearly three years on the job. He did not press enough on deadlines to suit Morgan, and Hearst approved her decision, noting in a telegram: "HIS EASY GOING WAYS HAVE COST US MANY THOUSAND DOLLARS WE NEED ENERGY SYSTEM AND DISCIPLINE."

Morgan selected Camille Rossi, who had worked for her in San Francisco during the past year, to take Washburn's place. Rossi worked at San Simeon for the next ten years and was responsible for general construction work and crews, maintenance of existing buildings and grounds, construction of supporting features such as pipelines, reservoirs, and power lines, and maintenance of construction equipment.

Hearst decided to begin work on La Casa Grande shortly after Rossi arrived. "Big pours" like La Casa Grande presented incredible challenges given the primitive construction methods of the day and the remote location. Cement and steel both had to be shipped by boat to San Simeon and stored in warehouses before horse-drawn teams hauled it up the steep grade. A crusher pulverized the rock excavated from the La Casa Grande site; water was piped in from natural springs. Sand from local beaches was washed free of salt and hauled to the hilltop. When a finer grade of cement was required, Morgan had fine white beach sand from Monterey or pumice substituted for the local sand.

As the supplies were gathered and transported, laborers built wooden forms to Morgan's specifications. In the days before pre-mix and concrete pumps, the

John Pellegrini, an Italian tile setter, recalled working at San Simeon in the 1920s:

> During Prohibition I used to go away for about two weeks, and I used to bring a big jug of wine [back to San Simeon]. Miss Morgan knew that [because] I told Miss Morgan one day, "Miss Morgan, I have to compromise with you." She said one word, "This is Prohibition." No liquor allowed on Hearst's place. But my men, they got to have their wine. It's like tea to an Englishman; otherwise, they don't stay there. They got to have their wine.

An aerial view of Hearst's remote hilltop estate shortly after the first towers on the main building were finished. Gathered in front of the main building are the three guest houses. At the extreme right are the tents and barracks of the construction camp.

cement mixer was stoked by hand; the fresh concrete was emptied into wheelbarrows and trundled to the forms in rapid succession by a fleet of laborers. Rossi's crews poured concrete continuously from August of 1922 to the spring of 1924 just to complete the two stories of the building as originally designed. During 1925 workers covered the exterior concrete with limestone facing from Utah; construction on the twin bell towers began the next year.

From the very beginning of the project, the design and decorative details of the main building preoccupied both Morgan and Hearst, a process that hardening concrete did not interrupt. The flow of drawings and telegrams between the two was punctuated by meetings in San Francisco and on-site. Walter Steilberg remembers the two deep in conversation many times amid hundreds of architectural volumes in her office library. Drafter Bjarne Dahl recalls Hearst pausing briefly to say hello to

staffers before joining Morgan, where "they would discuss everything about the building. And he would see all of the books together [in her office library], so when he went to Europe, they decided to get two books of each kind, if they could—one for his library and one for her library."

Both had consulted a 1917 volume on architecture in southern Spain by Austin Whittlesey that would inform much of Morgan's exterior detail on La Casa Grande. Early in 1920 Morgan wrote to Hearst about the facade and entrance to the main building: "I believe we could get something really very beautiful by using the combination of Ronda towers and the Sevilla doorway [as pictured in the Whittlesey book], with your Virgin over it and San Simeon and San Christophe on either side. This would allow for great delicacy and at the same time, brilliance in the decoration." Hearst agreed enthusiastically and plans went forward.

STUDY FOR LOWER HALL OF HOUSE A FOR
MR. WILLIAM RANDOLPH HEARST ——— SCALE AT WALL ½"=1'-0" ——— JULIA MORGAN ARCHITECT

Morgan made dozens of preliminary sketches such as this one, above, so that Hearst could approve the use and placement of his many works of art.

La Casa del Mar, left, was named for the breathtaking view of the Pacific available from its windows and terraces.

Julia Morgan's final sketch for the second tower design for La Casa Grande. The lower portion of the drawing indicates the window treatment for the Celestial Suite bedrooms, which were built on the site of the former pencil-shaped towers. Morgan directed the placement of water storage tanks and the bells for Hearst's custom-made carillon at the top.

Thousands of blueprints and architectural drawings still exist for San Simeon; many of them bear Hearst's handwritten opinions of Morgan's work as well as requests for changes and embellishments. Additional correspondence was sent through Hearst's executive secretary, Col. Joseph Willicombe.

A former reporter, Willicombe often served as Hearst's hatchet man, delivering unpopular news or decisions to employees of the Hearst Corporation, the ranch, and even family members. Willicombe's letters invariably began, "The Chief says . . ." and were ignored at the recipient's peril.

Hearst's ideas for La Casa Grande were so fluid that he sometimes requested changes even after the work had been successfully completed. In 1927 Hearst decided two additional wings at the rear of the building were necessary. The south (or service) wing was begun in the summer of 1927; a north wing (also called the recreation or new wing) at the end of 1929. As construction progressed on these additions, Hearst was then convinced that the view from the Doge's Suite in the main building had been marred. His solution was to order the exchange of the Doge's bedroom's fireplaces and the offending windows. Workers then began the expensive and difficult task of moving the functioning fireplaces and flues to the north and south walls of the bedrooms.

Also in 1929 Hearst proposed lifting the roof of the original structure to add a third floor to the center portion of the building. Further changes to the main building came when Hearst ordered the original towers redesigned to include a carillon, or set of stationary bells, each producing one tone in the chromatic scale by means of a keyboard. The pencil-shaped finials inspired by the Ronda cathedral were razed and the former towers were enclosed to create the Celestial Suite's bedrooms. New towers were then constructed above these bedrooms. Room was left in each tower for the bells and a 2,500-gallon water tank fed by gravity from the reservoir on a nearby peak.

The carillon was ordered from Michiels Brothers foundry in Tournai, Belgium, after Morgan wrote them on October 8, 1921:

Crates en route to Hearst's estate, left, were loaded onto trucks at the railroad station in San Luis Obispo for the journey up the coast to San Simeon's warehouses.

Above, a page from one of the many sketchbooks Julia Morgan filled on her trips abroad in search of architectural inspiration. Here she meticulously noted the design of various escutcheons, or shields bearing coats of arms. The "little lion" at right pleased Hearst and was used to great effect at San Simeon.

Mr. William Randolph Hearst is building a country estate in California, the site being on top of a mountain about 1,800 feet above the sea, and commanding the coast for miles, as well as range after range of mountains. There is a tiny ranch community about three miles below but no other habitation. The main building has two towers, an outline sketch of which is attached. He would like a carillon of the Belgian type of about 25 to 35 bells, sweet in tone, wide in range, operated by organ bench . . . at will. He is prepared to spend $25,000 for the bells. . . . As the bells are to serve a decorative, as well as musical purpose, they are to be hung in the openings of the towers, even though I know better effect could be obtained if hung in rows in one tower. . . .

After considerable delay, a 48-bell carillon for San Simeon was manufactured. But before the bells had cleared Customs, Hearst had second thoughts about adding them to the towers. Marcel Michiels' son and namesake, together with an assistant, had already arrived in California for the exacting process of installation and tuning, so Hearst allowed them to proceed. One range of twelve bells was never installed; the remaining thirty-six bells were halved and placed in both towers, despite the recommendations of the manufacturer. Hearst was never quite pleased with the tone, urging Morgan in 1934 to visit Holland on her European vacation so she could hear a carillon with the effect he wanted reproduced at San Simeon.

Hearst made other changes to La Casa Grande, many of which were never completed. In the early 1930s he requested a bowling alley in the basement directly underneath the movie theater. There was room for only two lanes, but Hearst wanted three. Maurice McClure (no relation to drafter Warren McClure), who first worked as a laborer at San Simeon, recalls Hearst saying to Morgan, as they were measuring the basement, "Well, Miss Morgan, move this wall over here another twelve feet." McClure remembered:

. . . After we had already dug the basement and had all these enormous foundations down there which were about the size of an automobile. . . .

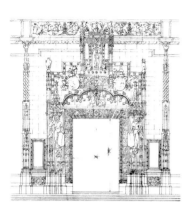

WEST ENTRANCE OF SAN SIMEON
[architectural drawing title block]

Morgan and Hearst deliberated at length over the main entrance to La Casa Grande, above. Morgan wrote, "I believe we could get something really very beautiful by using the combination of Ronda towers and the Sevilla doorway. . . ."

A rare view of La Casa Grande, right, made from a glass plate negative taken by a photographer Morgan hired to document progress on the hilltop. Hearst wrote in March of 1924: "The big house is a whale. If I had known it would be so big I would have made the little buildings bigger."

Opposite, Morgan's sketch for an art gallery at San Simeon, a structure which was never built. In addition, Hearst had plans for other amenities that were never realized, including a ballroom, banquet hall, and clock tower for the main building, plus a polo field, croquet lawn, topiary maze, a zoo building and aviary, and two more guest houses.

They had to take out the north wall, the full length of the main building, from the basement to up above ground level. Chip it out, [because] it was already cast in place. And modify some enormous reinforced concrete foundations underneath the basement floor, that would later support columns that would support loads clear up to the roof. And . . . moving the wall over some twelve feet, or whatever it was, affected the location of those columns as well. And so it was an enormous job to move that wall over to accommodate one more bowling alley [lane]. But it was done."

McClure estimated the cost of moving the wall at $45,000. The bowling alley was never built.

Morgan accepted these and other changes to the San Simeon estate from her unpredictable client with her characteristic calm, drew new plans, and billed Hearst for the changes. Although Hearst sometimes chafed at delays, there is no record that Morgan ever responded in kind, an astonishing, even saintly, feat for a working relationship that lasted nearly three decades.

During the early stages of construction, Hearst alerted Morgan to the preferences of Millicent Hearst and his five sons. Passionate as he was about it, San Simeon began as a country house in contrast to his primary residence in New York. But by the mid-1920s Hearst found little reason to stay in New York with his political ambitions in ashes and his marriage cooling. He returned to San Simeon for increasingly longer periods of time, usually with actress Marion Davies as his companion. His wife Millicent maintained a luxury flat in Manhattan and her Long Island estate at Sands Point, traveling only infrequently to California. A great deal of her time was taken up with the Free Milk Fund for Babies, a charitable organization she had founded.

La Casa Grande was under construction steadily from 1922 to 1937 and from 1945 to 1947, not counting the earliest period of time when rock was blasted for the foundations. By 1947, when Hearst was forced to stop making changes, La Casa Grande, the center-piece of San Simeon, rose 137 feet from the main terrace to the top of the bell

towers. The main house had approximately 115 rooms on four floors and nearly 60,000 square feet of living space. Julia Morgan's design provided Hearst's guests with twenty-six bedrooms, thirty-two bathrooms, fourteen sitting rooms, a main library, a mammoth dining hall, thirty fireplaces, a billiard room, and a sumptuous movie theater with a projection booth.

Hearst moved from his quarters in La Casa del Mar to the main building, sharing a private suite of rooms on his newly added third floor with Marion Davies. On October 9, 1928, Morgan wrote, "The elevator machinery is all installed and operating, and the carpenters are putting the woodwork of the cab in. You will be able to step in, press the Gothic Suite button, and not be surprised to find moved up there a good many of your fine things—it is really scrumptious up there." The Gothic Suite included a relatively small and modestly decorated bedroom for himself, a handsome sitting room overlooking the Pacific, a second bedroom for Davies, and two baths.

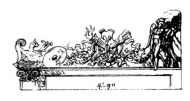

HEARST AS AN EMPLOYER
Gardener Norman Rotanzi, who began work for Hearst in 1934, recalled:
> He had a . . . unique method of motivating people. When he got through talking to you, you felt like you were part of the Hearst Corporation, and you'd say to yourself: 'Well, he's the kind of guy I'd like to do a good day's work for.'

Waiter Fred Redelsperger remembers:
> The thing that impressed me about him is that he knew the first name of a lot of those people who didn't realize he knew their first name. The guys that brought the papers up from San Luis. "Is So-and-So in?" "Yes." "Are the papers in?" He called down there one day. . . . He was a very astute man.

Zoo worker Hayes Perkins commented:
> Seeing so much of Hearst at short range I do not marvel he is considered one of the greatest men of his time. Were it not for his companions he might easily win his way into the affections of the American people, for he is a kindly man at heart. Perhaps he loves praise, for those with him are constantly flattering him to gain his favor.

And business owner Zel Bordegary reflected:
> I always felt rather afraid of him because he was an important man and I always had this feeling that everyone that surrounded him was somewhat afraid of Mr. Hearst. I mean, he could make or break you and if you didn't do as you were told, why, you could be just [sent] right down off that hill.

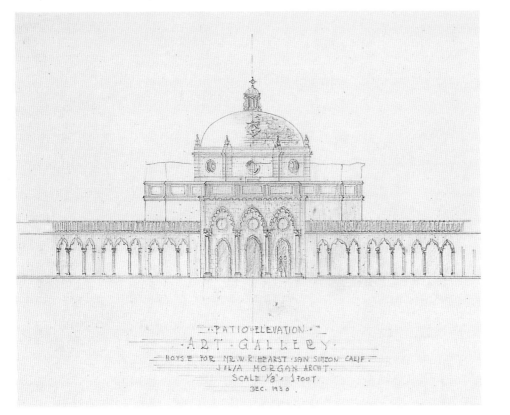

·PATIO·ELEVATION·
·ART·GALLERY·
HOUSE FOR MR. W. R. HEARST SAN SIMEON CALIF.
JULIA MORGAN ARCH'T.
SCALE 1/8" = 1 FOOT.
DEC. 1930

Dressed in riding clothes, Millicent Hearst, above, inspects a thirteenth-century carved marble piece in the courtyard of La Casa del Sol.

Key members of Hearst's staff at San Simeon, including the maintenance supervisor, head gardener, and construction superintendent, were rewarded with charming Morgan-designed stucco houses on the bay in the village of San Simeon. Some of the best examples of her domestic vernacular style, the houses were built only after Morgan had consulted at length with each family to determine their habits and wishes.

Directly across the hall is the suitably imposing Gothic Library, the command post of his media empire and repository of his finest books and manuscripts.

The service wing of La Casa Grande added twelve more bedrooms, ten bathrooms, a hotel-sized kitchen and pantries, a staff dining room, and seven utility rooms to the total for the main house. The 9,000-square-foot basement contains nine vaults, a wine cellar, walk-in coolers, storage for linen, glassware, and china, and a boiler room. Hearst had a barber's chair installed in the service wing for the comfort of his guests when a hairdresser or dentist were needed.

Hearst also enlisted Morgan's services for his Northern California estate, Wyntoon, in the mid-1920s. Inherited from his mother, Wyntoon covered 50,000 acres along the winding McCloud River near Mount Shasta. Phoebe Hearst's enormous house, designed by Bernard Maybeck with Morgan's help in 1902, burned during the winter of 1929–1930. Hearst decided to rebuild immediately and commanded more and more of Morgan's time for Wyntoon. In Morgan's wake came a platoon of construction workers, household help, gardeners, chauffeurs, and cooks, often drafted from their duties at San Simeon for as long as Hearst would be in residence.

As Hearst's plans for San Simeon and Wyntoon expanded continually, Morgan needed an architectural drafter at the San Simeon site at all times. On October 9, 1929, Hearst wrote, "When you are not here, and when we have no one representing you that I can confer with or have confidence in, I am asked about things that I know very little about, and I do not like to make decisions except on general matters. . . . I do not think an architect and an engineer would cost any more than the two architects we had for awhile, and if they did cost more, what is the difference? This is a big work and justifies a big organization."

At Hearst's request, Warren McClure, who had worked for Morgan on Hearst's Beverly Hills mansion, began work at San Simeon in January of 1930. McClure recalled:

I was Miss Morgan's man on the job. She did not stay there but made one-day visits every week or so. My little shack office was in the east court [yard] and WRH would spend hours in it every day. I recall Miss Davies popping in at times with the question, "What are you kids cooking up now?" The "cooking up" was usually something akin to the Vatican or Windsor Castle to the later disconcerting of Miss Morgan and the treasury. None told him nay. . . . Part

of the setup was to have a draftsman with some designing ability at hand to get the ideas given by Mr. Hearst on paper, which were forwarded to Miss Morgan's office in San Francisco.

Hearst was pleased with Warren McClure's work and had him travel between San Simeon and Wyntoon throughout the 1930s. During World War II, McClure was on hand at Wyntoon or the Santa Monica beach house to capture Hearst's ideas for future building. After the war Warren McClure implemented the last of the changes to San Simeon for Morgan, following Hearst to Beverly Hills in 1948 and working there until 1951.

During C. C. Rossi's ten-year span at the estate from 1922 to 1932, considerable work was done on landscaping. Morgan planned a broad, U-shaped esplanade to link the four buildings for strolling guests. Grading the walkway on the uneven hilltop was time-consuming, as was enlarging the terrace below La Casa del Sol, which Rossi's crews also began.

For those who preferred riding to walking, Hearst requested a pergola, an arbor-like affair of colonnades supporting open rafters. Nearly a thousand espaliered fruit trees and climbing vines were added to the structure, according to the design of landscape architect Bruce Porter, whom Morgan used as a consultant. Hearst's pergola was bigger and higher than most, coursing over a mile around the hillside. Morgan took special care to build the colonnades and crosspieces high enough so that Hearst, a tall man who favored large hats, could canter with ease on his favorite horse under its shelter.

Although Rossi was prolific in the amount of work that was produced, his tenure at San Simeon was never smooth. According to Bjarne Dahl, plumber Alex

Rankin, Maurice McClure, and others, Rossi often attempted to circumvent Morgan by cultivating Hearst directly. He was consistently reprimanded by Morgan for acting on his own and refusing to cooperate. According to Rankin, Rossi began to carry a gun on the job because "his men were about to wrap a two-by-four around his head."

Of the work on the indoor pool in 1932, tile setter Joseph Giarritta recalled:

> [Rossi] and his family lived in one of the homes near the ocean [in San Simeon village]. Every morning, he would drive up to the hilltop. He was in charge of construction, but not the craftsmen, like plumbers, painters, plasterers, and the [tile setters for the] Roman Pool. He was a good engineer but a little overbearing. He wasn't very popular with the men
>
> Miss Morgan gave orders that no work was to be done on the pool unless she okayed it. [When] Miss Morgan wasn't there Mr. Rossi had his men pour the concrete on the right and left stairs leading to the dive platform and on the diving platform itself. When Miss Morgan came back and saw what Mr. Rossi had done, she was livid. She was a small woman, but she sure could get angry.

> Miss Morgan had the laborers chop out all the concrete [and] wooden frames, and build them over again. . . . The fact that Mr. Rossi went against her orders sure stirred her up. He was trying to undermine her influence with Mr. Hearst, which was impossible. She was so incensed with Mr. Rossi that she had signs put on the doors leading to the pools, such as, "Mr. Rossi, under no circumstances are you to enter this pool." He never came in after that.

Rossi had crossed Morgan for the final time. Shortly after this incident he was permanently dismissed by Morgan with Hearst's blessing. He attempted to retain his job by appealing directly to Hearst. Despite Rossi's importunate letter, Morgan was firm in her decision, reminding Hearst that Rossi "is so unduly revengeful and finds so many ingenious ways for indirect expression of his sentiments." Morgan concluded, "I may be unreasonably tired of operating with a constant sense of contrary purpose, and not see conditions fairly or clearly as your fresh eye can." Rossi found another job with Morgan's help.

Morgan had faced a similar situation ten years before with head gardener H. Dodson Hazard, who refused to

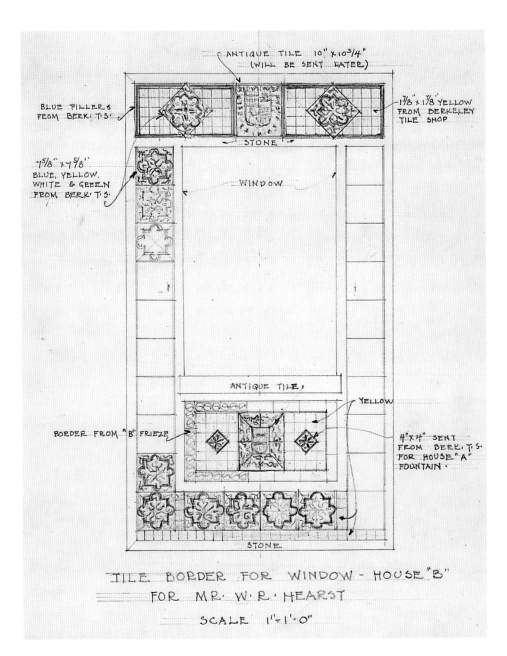

ANTIQUE TILE 10" X 10¾"
(WILL BE SENT LATER)

BLUE FILLERS
FROM BERK. T. S.

1⅛" x 1⅛" YELLOW
FROM BERKELEY
TILE SHOP

7⅝" x 7⅝"
BLUE, YELLOW,
WHITE & GREEN
FROM BERK. T. S.

STONE

WINDOW

ANTIQUE TILE,

YELLOW

BORDER FROM "B" FRIEZE

4" X 4" SENT
FROM BERK. T. S.
FOR HOUSE "A"
FOUNTAIN.

STONE

TILE BORDER FOR WINDOW – HOUSE "B"
FOR MR. W. R. HEARST
SCALE 1" = 1'-0"

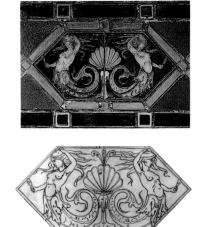

Morgan designed virtually everything at San Simeon, including individual tiles for window borders, left, and exterior details, above. The mermaid theme tile is shown in its completed form, top.

share information with her or comply with simple requests. In March of 1922 Hazard wrote an inflammatory letter to Morgan, which included the following passage:

> *I would advise that the lay-outs, buying, and planting of Ornamental and Fruit-stock, and the designing of Vistas on this place has been worked out by Mr. Hearst with me, and the matter entrusted to my care. The work has been progressing satisfactorily under almost "impossible" conditions, and shall continue to progress until stopped by my Chief, Mr. W. R. Hearst.*

Morgan wrote to Hearst, saying, "Enclosed is a letter from Hazard which explains itself, in a sense." She continued in a mild vein, noting, "I think Hazard tried very hard to please you, and for that reason I have humored him along although some time ago he told me that 'his department on your orders' had, and would have, nothing whatever to do with me or my office people." Morgan disciplined Hazard and work progressed, but in April of 1925 Morgan sent Hearst word of Hazard's threat to resign "for the fifth time since last summer." This time Morgan accepted the resignation and replaced him in short order.

Fairmont Hotel, which Morgan was rehabilitating after the great fire and earthquake. A reporter asked him, "Is the building really in the charge of a woman architect?" His forceful reply: "This building is in the charge of a *real* architect and her name happens to be Julia Morgan."

Many accounts exist of Morgan's nerveless ability to inspect construction sites top to bottom, climbing ladders and scaffolding in her trademark tailored suits. Longtime Morgan employee Walter Steilberg once admitted to fear in following her when he arrived at her office on the fourteenth floor of San Francisco's Merchant's Exchange Building one morning to find "a ladder in the library leaning out of the window to a suspended scaffold." Soon Morgan appeared coming back down the ladder "quite a-glow with enthusiasm [for the work in progress and] urged me to go up on the scaffold and see for myself. It was a fearful experience; but I went, conquering my trembling."

Morgan found the construction superintendent she desired in George Loorz, the third person to assume the job. He bossed San Simeon from 1932 to 1937 on-site, and indirectly until 1940. Loorz, a Berkeley alumnus, started working with Morgan in 1926 on Wyntoon, Hearst's Northern California estate. Pleased with the quality of his work on the pool and tennis courts, Morgan next sent Loorz to finish similar work at Marion Davies' mammoth Ocean House in Santa Monica.

Under Morgan's direction at San Simeon, Loorz's crews finished the indoor (or Roman) pool, the pergola, the expansion of "C" Terrace beneath La Casa del Sol, and the enlargement of the Neptune Pool, including the addition of colonnades and Greek temple facade. He supervised the addition of new baths and dressing rooms in the north wing, and worked closely with artisans on the installation of many ceilings and other

Rossi and Hazard were certainly not the only people who doubted her ability, but Morgan usually won the respect and loyalty of laborers and professionals alike with a combination of skill and thoroughness. Her ability was defended as early as 1906 by the construction superintendent of San Francisco's

works of art. He also implemented Morgan's plans for the Milpitas Hacienda, a complete, if smaller, ranch complex at the northern end of the San Simeon ranch, near Jolon, California.

George Loorz recalled the challenge of hard physical labor that construction at San Simeon required, particularly under Frank Souza. "[He] ran a tough crew. . . He was a tough Portuguese labor foreman, believe me. His men *worked*. If anyone came there with the idea that this was Mr. Hearst and you didn't have to work, brother, they didn't last long with Frank." Brayton Laird, a laborer on "Babe" Souza's crew, remembers being invited to the nightly movie screening, but "nine times out of ten your back was so broken that at nine o'clock you were sound asleep around here. It was a rough go. [Souza] used to push those men, boy, he made them work.

It was tough to work up here. They didn't pay top scale [to unskilled workers] either."

In 1937 Loorz finished the bunkhouse on the horse ranch at the bottom of the hill, ending his on-site supervision at San Simeon because of Hearst's looming financial crisis. Loorz had arrived at San Simeon with the understanding that he could continue with his outside firm, the F. C. Stolte Co., on buildings on the Central Coast and in the San Joaquin Valley. Loorz recollected, "The only rule he [Hearst] made was, 'Where can we get in touch with you?' And he'd call. It was nothing for him to call at one o'clock in the morning and ask you the simplest question."

Construction on San Simeon halted completely during World War II when building supplies and laborers were unavailable. Maurice McClure was a

The third and final incarnation of the outdoor swimming pool at San Simeon.

One of hundreds of truckloads of mature trees on their way to San Simeon to transform the barren hillsides.

construction laborer on the hilltop from 1926 until January of 1931, when he became a member of the household staff. He returned to Berkeley in 1933 for an engineering degree. In August of 1945 McClure returned to San Simeon as construction superintendent at George Loorz's request. During this period Julia Morgan was consulted infrequently as she was travelling much of the time, so Maurice McClure took his direction from Warren A. McClure, an architectural drafter in Morgan's office who had represented her on-site since 1930.

Most of the work on San Simeon during the post-war period was concentrated on the recreation wing, where a third floor was added and interior work was completed on bedrooms and bathrooms. Maurice McClure also supervised the paving of the road up the hilltop, expanding the service wing, and building a paved runway and new hangar at the ranch airport at the bottom of the hill.

Much attention has been paid to the construction process on the hilltop, but an equal amount of demanding physical labor was necessary to landscape the vast area to Hearst's wishes. Morgan, as usual, was at the heart of the design process to convert the arid rocky bluffs into a horticultural wonderland.

Coast live oak, cañon or maul oak, California scrub oak, valley oak, pin oak, and cork oak are all present on the hilltop. The native coast live oaks (*Quercus agrifolia*) were inviolable to Hearst. It is believed that one of this species, hundreds of years old, was cut down during early construction; the act so disturbed Hearst that he decreed no further trees would be lost. In the 1920s and early 1930s, three oaks were moved short distances to accommodate the main building site plan. Another oak was moved in 1946 so that branches would not have to be cut when the service wing was enlarged. Saving these oaks called on Morgan's knowledge of civil engineering, the advice of tree specialists, the muscle of both landscaping and construction crews, and the services of house movers and their equipment.

The moving process took six months and cost about $18,000 for each tree. A concrete cradle two to three inches thick was poured into a trench dug around the drip line of the tree. While workers excavated a new hole nearby, the house movers used their equipment to jack the tree and its roots up out of the earth. Workers then separated the roots from the earth with timbering. Giant logs were placed underneath the timbering to roll the tree to the new site. Careful watch was kept on each tree's root system and consistent moisture was applied so that the roots pushed through the holes and eventually broke the concrete cradle.

During 1929 Hearst himself monitored "the two fine trees which [we] moved to the north terrace." He wrote to Morgan, "My private opinion is that tree surgeons are a lot of fakes anyhow. I believe that our own people could do everything that they do and do it better." The trees thrived in their new locations, but three of the four have been lost to storms or disease in the last decade.

Hearst was not a man to delay on important matters nor was he content

Professional house-movers, hired by Julia Morgan, use their equipment to move a centuries-old oak tree to a new location.

Mexican fan palm trees were used in several locations on the hilltop. Here workers place fifteen-foot palms near La Casa del Monte.

The garden pathway leading to the Neptune Pool is shaded by a coast live oak.

to see his gardens and trees mature from seeds and saplings. While major construction was underway, grounds worker Brayton Laird remembers, "All over the county they would pick up these big palms in people's yards, or cypress trees and bring them up here."

Thirty-three Italian cypress (*Cupressus sempervirens*) trees were purchased from an astonished homeowner in Adelaida, outside Paso Robles, on the other side of the Santa Lucia mountains. Mr. Claassen recalled, "In 1928 Mr. Hearst stopped by my home and asked if I would be willing to sell the 28- to 30-foot tall cypress. He offered me ten dollars each and said he would pay me to care for them until they were ready to ship. I was most happy with the arrange-

ment [because] the trees were already too big for [my] house."

"I was the one that was in charge of the balling and hauling of the cypress," remembers ranch employee Stanley Heaton. "It took us well onto two years from the time we started" to box them, ensure the tap roots had taken hold, and get them to San Simeon. Three of the tall trees fit on a truck at a time. They were hauled down to San Luis Obispo after traffic was halted on the Cuesta Grade and then fifty more miles to the hilltop.

The towering Mexican fan palms (*Washingtonia robusta*) that front La Casa Grande were rescued from the aftermath of the disastrous Berkeley fire of 1923. The untouched trees were excavated and moved by barge from Oakland to San Simeon.

In 1935 Hearst ordered citrus trees densely planted around the base of the Neptune Pool. He was advised that they would be planted too close together, but the publisher replied he was "getting up in years" and wanted a dense planting immediately. Gardeners solved the problem by pruning the trees into a continuous citrus hedge rather than thinning them.

Brayton Laird also remembers the backbreaking work of men and horses to plant an incredible 6,335 pines on a hill east of the main building, blasting four-foot holes for each of the trees out of rock. About five miles distant and 2,000 feet higher than "Camp Hill," this peak was selected by Morgan as the site for the reservoir; Hearst decided a grove of pines would transform the hill while screening the reservoir from view. Soil then had to be brought from San Simeon Point up to the barren site "by truckload, shoveling it the hard way . . . into the trees when we planted," recollects Laird. Horses were used to pull the trees to the site on wooden sleds.

Each tree "would weigh anywhere from a ton to a ton-and-a-half. And we would lower them in the hole and then we'd water them in and we'd have big basins that had to be watered two or three times during the summer," Laird remembers. "We had enough lumber laying around [from the discarded sleds] to build a small town, so we had to take all that lumber and store it down in gullies to keep it out of sight." Similar efforts were made to establish sequoias (*Sequoiadendron gigantea*) at the cowboy camp in a canyon near Burnett Peak, the highest point on the ranch. About half of the sequoia trees survive today.

Orchards were planted near the pergola, which meant more blasting. Five sticks of dynamite were used per hole and fifteen were detonated at a time. "You could hear them all down to

San Simeon and all over . . . Maybe ten to fifteen times a day," Brayton Laird recalls. "Our instructions were never to blast before 9:30 AM when Hearst was on the hill. Well, one night the party came in and we didn't know it and we'd just set off about forty-five or fifty of them by 9:30. Here comes Marion Davies' bodyguard. . . . He comes running down there and he thought we were being attacked by the Japanese."

Plum, cherry, apple, and peach trees were planted in the orchards. There were also many varieties of citrus trees on the hilltop, including tangelo, lime, lemon, grapefruit, kumquat, tangerine, and Panama, Mandarin, and sweet oranges. Avocado, quince, persimmon, loquat, fig, olive, pomegranate, and walnut trees were added as well.

Workers were forbidden to pick or eat fruit from trees on the hilltop for themselves because Hearst enjoyed the ornamental effect of the ripe fruit. When the orchard crews picked fruit in the orchards once a week, it was used in the Casa Grande and construction camp kitchens and distributed in the village of San Simeon. Hearst had excess fruit, estimated at a thousand dozen per year, packed in specially labeled crates and shipped as gifts far and wide. Kitchen staff and women from the village made jellies and jams each year. Two tons of walnuts were also harvested and distributed from the Hearst orchards each year.

Every tree planted or growing on Hearst's ranch was the responsibility of transplanted Englishman Nigel Keep, who remained with Hearst from the early 1920s until his retirement in 1948. Keep was working at a nursery in the San Francisco Bay area when Hearst arrived to purchase some trees. Keep advised Hearst against the purchase of some inferior stock, earning Hearst's lasting affection and a new job. Apart from Morgan, Hearst seldom encountered individuals concerned about saving him money.

Keep, who preferred the title of

Hearst greatly respected head gardener Nigel Keep, who secured a lifetime position with Hearst when he saved the publisher money on tree purchases. When he was 83 and Keep 72, Hearst sent this photo with the handwritten inscription: "Dear Mr. Keep— This is a good picture of two very handsome young men."

Opposite the entrance to La Casa del Sol stands the marble group The Three Graces, *right. Representing Zeus' three daughters, Brilliance, Joy, and Bloom, the work was sculpted by Boyer after Antonio Canova. The life-sized bronze statue* Adam and Eve, *above, was acquired from sculptor Arthur George Walker in 1930.*

"tree-planter" to any other, enjoyed a degree of respect from his coworkers second only to Julia Morgan herself. Longtime gardener Norman Rotanzi, who worked with Nigel Keep, recalled:

> *Mr. Keep was a very fine gentleman. He was a perfectionist. He wasn't a slave driver. . . . He wanted quality work. He was a very interesting man to work with and he knew the botanical name of every tree. . . . If anyone wanted to learn anything about horticulture, this was really their opportunity in those days.*

Of Keep's devotion to his work, Brayton Laird remembered:

> *Mr. Keep was very very strict on not hurting the tree. They were all like little children to him. On the cold mornings he liked the lizards that protected the trees, eat[ing] the bugs and everything, so he'd*

> *keep them warm, and keep them in his shirt, a whole bunch of lizards. And then we had [problems with] gophers. He was after the gophers all the time, and if we ever killed a gopher snake, that was curtains for us.*

Norman Rotanzi began work at San Simeon in 1934, became head gardener in 1948, and continued there until his death in 1992. He remembered W. R. Hearst as

> *. . . a brilliant man. He knew all the names of the plants and most of the pests we have to deal with. The gardeners were sort of his pets. He would like to come out and stroll around the gardens and talk to everybody. And it didn't make any difference who he had with him . . . Winston Churchill, or the president of U. S. Steel, or whoever it was, he would*

SCALE ¼"=1'0"

SUGGESTION FOR FEATURE OPPOSITE ENTRANCE OF HOUSE B

always introduce you to these people . . . and when they got to know you, they would walk by and call you by your first name.

As Morgan's attention was devoted more and more to construction and design matters, she delegated responsibility for the landscaping to Gardiner Dailey, who was trained in her San Francisco office. But he was removed after Hearst sent Morgan a terse telegram: "DAILEY WE DO NOT NEED." She then relied on horticulturalist Isabella Worn, who traveled to San Simeon intermittently from 1926 through the mid-1930s, to plan the arrangement and color coordination of the flowering plants. Bruce Porter, who had designed the pergola landscaping, completed the plans for Hearst's massive tree-planting projects on the ranch.

In 1920 Morgan also hired a head gardener to implement the landscaping plans. She began with Dodson Hazard, who stayed for five years, until his dismissal for lack of cooperation. The turnover in this position continued. Albert Webb, Fred Macklin, Henry Reesing, and James Chatfield succeeded Dailey in the 1920s and early 1930s. Only when Nigel Keep was appointed as head of grounds and orchards in the mid-1930s was Hearst completely satisfied.

From the first days of construction, Hearst fired off orders to Morgan for thousands of flowers. Hearst's earliest plans for San Simeon, dating to the request for a single house, specified a large rose garden. On January 19, 1921, Hearst wired Morgan:

PROCEED WITH PLANTING ALSO BUY OTHER PLANTS AND TREES NEEDED CAN YOU SEND ME SKETCHES OF COLOR FLORAL SCHEME FOR HOUSES FOR INSTANCE SUPPOSE WE HAVE WHITE AND PINK CLIMBING ROSES FOR ENTRANCE SIDE OF HOUSE A, RED ROSES FOR B, YELLOW ROSES FOR C, WITH PURPLE BOURGOUVILLAS [SIC] FOR TOWERS OF C ETCETERA LAY OUT SOME DEFINITE PLANS AND COLOR COMBINATIONS

Morgan's sketch, labeled "Suggestions for Feature Opposite Entrance of House B" includes the Hearst- and Morgan-like figures at left. The bench sketched in at center was replaced with a third-century Roman marble sarcophagus depicting Apollo and the Nine Muses.

On Monday, January 24, Morgan responded by letter:

> . . . I had planned to go down tonight, taking a good working gardener to prepare the beds, but San Simeon reports a heavy storm on. There is a lot of work to do getting proper soil up [to the hilltop] and in. I would like to send you a little model of each house with the plantings around, but spoiled the "C" model in the effort to show the plantings in detail and have had to have it recast. I will try photographing the model from different viewpoints and coloring the prints. If you find this helpful, we can do the other houses, starting the actual planting on "C" first.

At the peak of hilltop operation, five greenhouses, designed by Morgan and located down the hillside near the construction camp, were in use. Because Hearst liked to see a complete change of the gardens for each season, three greenhouses and two gardeners were devoted to the propagation of 700,000 annuals year-round. Even this operation did not satisfy each season's need for annuals, so orders were filled from nurseries in the San Francisco Bay area.

Hearst was in the habit of carrying wheat in his pocket to feed large flocks of quail during his strolls about the grounds. Gardeners would spend an entire day planting thousands of annuals, but would return the next morning to find hundreds of plants missing. Close observation revealed that the birds were pulling the flowers out of the gardens. When Nigel Keep explained the quail problem to Hearst, he merely replied, "Well, Mr. Keep, you'll just have to raise more annuals!"

George Loorz remembered Portuguese gardener Alfredo Gomes, who

> became very popular with Mr. Hearst because he was a specialist in flowers and those two [additional] greenhouses down

> there were built for him, actually. . . . He watered and bossed those two greenhouses. They were beautiful, those begonias and gloxinia. They were the most beautiful thing on the hill. . . . He didn't want anyone to water those flowers but him. And a funny thing about it, was that most of those people that were temperamental like that were the very best. . . . There were some pretty talented people who were hard workers.

As late as 1932 Hearst was still personally reviewing the list of bulbs slated for purchase. He chided one head gardener, writing, "The effects and the variety and proportion of extra beautiful flowers do not seem to have been as satisfactory as in previous years. . . . If some favored florist gets the idea that we are regular customers no matter what they send us, we will naturally not get the best results. I find in my experience that that is the case no matter how big or how little the institution with which I deal. Anyone from the paper manufacturer to the butcher has to be carefully watched to see that they deliver at the highest standards."

Rotanzi remembered how Hearst enjoyed discussing gardening and flowers with Keep's crew after lunch, but "many times the valet would come out and inform Mr. Hearst of a telephone call. . . . If it wasn't anyone of importance, he would tell that valet to tell the caller that he was outside gardening with the boys," and would return the call later. Morgan's phone calls were the only exception to this rule.

By the mid-1930s the windswept and rocky "Camp Hill" had been changed beyond recognition. The phenomenal efforts of Morgan and her construction and landscaping crews had transformed the hilltop into the miniature Mediterranean village Hearst had always pictured.

Hearst envisioned his gardens as further opportunities to display works of art from his vast collections. Amid the hedged Japanese boxwood and flowering trees of the gardens, opposite, stands the marble sculpture Europa, by German artist Fritz Behn.

(Overleaf) Architect Julia Morgan's attention to detail is evident in this painstaking design for the mosaic in the loggia of La Casa del Mar.

FACE OF MOSAIC

ONE

FRENCH WINDOWS.   FRENCH

FINISHED LOGGIA

11-3

MOSAIC

[LOOKING

FOR MR WILLIA

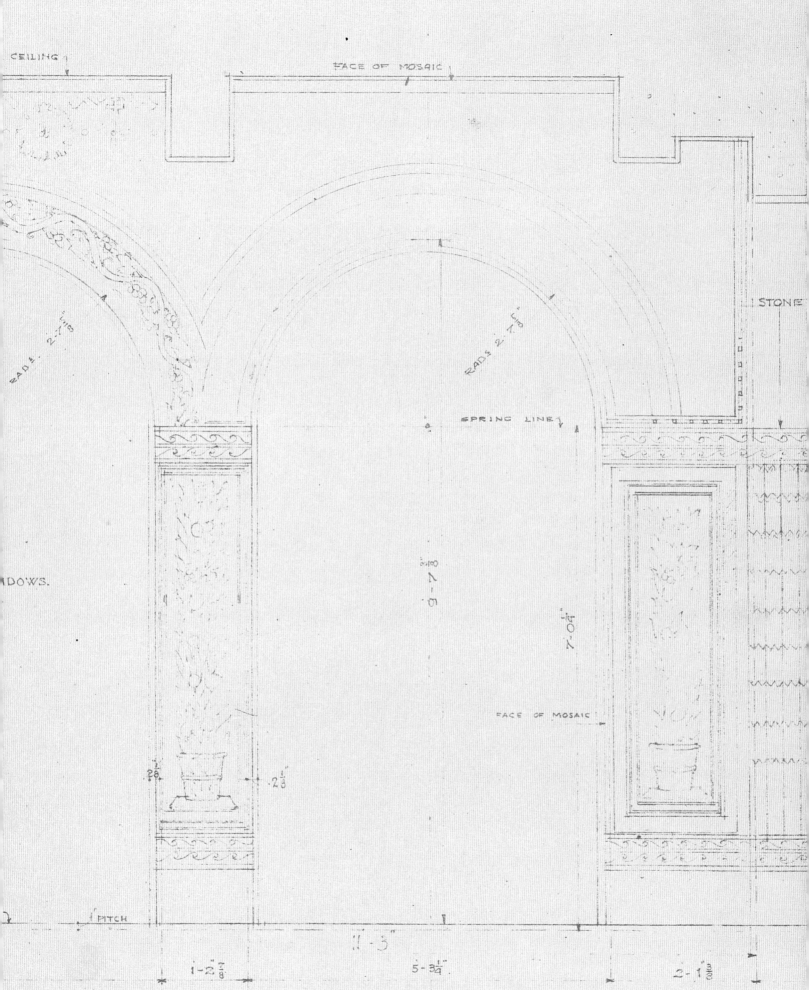

CEILING

FACE OF MOSAIC

10

5-8

10

1-1

10

STONE

RADS. 2'-7⅝"

RADS 2'-7"

SPRING LINE

DOWS.

FACE OF MOSAIC

PITCH

11'-3"

1-2⅞"

5-3¼"

2-1⅜"

TO PLASTER

LOGGIA. (HOUSE A).

YARDS HALL.

RANDOLPH HEARST.

CHAPTER THREE

*Gathering His
Greatest Pleasures:
Art & Architecture*

A s San Simeon grew, Julia Morgan found herself increasingly involved in the operation, as well as the design, of the estate. Funds from William Randolph Hearst flowed through her office for the purchase of everything from Egyptian statues and Hoover vacuum cleaners to raw meat for the polar bears in the hilltop zoo. Early in 1920 Morgan wrote to Hearst of an "actual cash deficit over the 6% commission" in his account, noting, "If the loss had been caused by the architectural work I would not have spoken of it but it is due to the expense of 'running the job,' as it were." Morgan biographer Sara Holmes Boutelle writes:

> *"Running the job" included hiring, firing, and settling disputes; arranging lodging, food, and working quarters for the laborers; making trips to interview specialists such as a cheese maker, a chicken man, gardeners, and housekeepers; procuring special plants and materials; creating various crafts centers on site; arranging transportation by ship, rail, and truck to the remote hilltop; building warehouses and cataloging objects to be incorporated in the project; checking on thousands of details; and satisfying the whims of artists and the client. That all this was taken care of by the architect was most unusual, but the physical remoteness of the site and the rare sense of partnership between architect and client in a venture cherished by both made it work. . . .*

By the early 1920s the flood of Hearst's art purchases from Europe became so great that Morgan assigned members of her staff to San Simeon to work exclusively on the seemingly endless deliveries. Hearst set up a similar operation in New York City, the International Studio Art Corporation, in an attempt to document his collections and smooth the path through Customs.

*THE ROMAN POOL
W. R. Hearst's desire for a "winter pool" resulted in Morgan's design for a "Roman Plunge." Every surface of the indoor swimming pool, opposite—including basin, walls, and ceiling—is covered in mosaics of hammered gold and delicate Venetian glass tiles. Details of the mosaic designs include stylized marine creatures, above left.*

Under architect Julia Morgan's direction, artisans often duplicated art objects from Hearst's voluminous collections. These "little lions," as Hearst called them, await their cast stone shields in the hilltop workshop. They are the first art pieces visitors to the hilltop usually see.

Of Hearst's purchases, Morgan wrote in November of 1921 to art dealers Arthur and Mildred Stapely Byne in Madrid:

So far we have received from him . . . some twelve or thirteen [railroad] carloads of antiques, brought from the ends of the earth and from prehistoric down to late Empire in period. . . . They comprise vast quantities of tables, beds, armoires, secretaires, all kinds of cabinets, polychrome church statuary, columns, door frames, carved doors . . . , over-altars, reliquaries, lanterns, iron grille doors, window grilles, votive candlesticks, torcheres, . . . six or seven well heads, marble and wood columns and door trims, a few good wooden carved ceilings . . . , a marble sanctuary arch from the entrance to some choir, and pictures . . . a number of Donatellos, lots of Della Robbias.

I don't see myself where we are ever going to use half suitably, but I find that the idea is to try things out and if they are not satisfactory, discard them for the next thing that comes. . . .

One railroad employee in San Luis Obispo (who also worked at San Simeon) recalls, "I helped them [un]load all that stuff: great big tapestries, mural pictures, you know, it'd take up the whole big car." Brayton Laird also remembers, "here was maybe a million dollars' worth of antiques and they would release it as household goods at 10¢ a pound. I don't know how they ever got by. If they'd had any damage they would have had an awful mess."

After being inventoried, art objects were placed in storage in a series of Morgan-designed warehouses near George Hearst's wharf against the day that Hearst would remember the purchase and want to include it in one of his houses. Some items were unearthed and sent to Hollywood for use on movie sets or to other cities for loan to museums. Still other shipments were never uncrated.

W. R. Hearst, like many other wealthy collectors of his day, was able to indulge in his enthusiasm for art and art collecting with virtually no restraints. International Harvester founder James Deering enjoyed importing entire rooms from abroad and reassembling them at Vizcaya, his Florida estate. Henry Ford moved houses of several famous Americans to his Greenfield Village outside Detroit, an early example of a living history park devoted to American history and culture. Henry E. Huntington, with whom Hearst sometimes competed for purchases, gathered a stunning array of books, manuscripts, and artwork at his home outside Pasadena, California. The collections formed by Andrew Mellon, the Rockefeller family, Isabella Stewart Gardner, the Vanderbilt family, Henry Clay Frick, and J. P. Morgan matched the quality, if not the quantity, of Hearst's collections.

Most of these notable nineteenth-century American *nouveaux riches* had more than a love of art motivating their acquisitions. Decorating their estates with art and antiquities lent the newly wealthy prestige and respectability, required large sums of discretionary income, and displayed their taste and discernment. In his typical fashion, Hearst exhibited these traits of his peers and often exceeded them, envisioning his collections primarily for his own pleasure and actual use.

Hearst asked Morgan to incorporate his collections into the function as well as the form of the residence. The publisher had not only San Simeon as his display case, but also Wyntoon, a village of Bavarian-styled chalets surrounded by 50,000 acres in northern California; a triplex in Manhattan; a million-acre ranch in Mexico; a fourteenth-century castle in Wales; a hundred-room "beach house" in Santa Monica; and several houses in Beverly Hills. All of these houses inspired the collector in Hearst, who rapidly filled them with even more treasures.

Phoebe Hearst, who had fostered her son's love of art and collecting since childhood, bequeathed to him prized pieces from her own vast collections of art, including sculpture, paintings, and books. The purchases Hearst made to augment these holdings were sometimes based on dealers' recommendations, but he customarily relied on his own knowledge of the field. He bought through most of the well-known auction houses, agents, and antique dealers in London and New York, including Sotheby's, Joseph Duveen, Christie's, French & Co., American Art Association, Parke-Bernet, and Anderson Galleries.

Some art and antiquities dealers, most notably Arthur and Mildred Stapley Byne, went to Europe armed with lists of his specific desires. Hearst complained bitterly about the frequent rise in price once his name was mentioned, so he often used an agent, anonymous bidding, or Morgan's office to make purchases. Mountains of art catalogs, which he perused thoroughly, were directed to him by hopeful galleries and auction houses. On occasion, he even drafted employees of the Hearst Corporation who worked in Great Britain into his perpetual hunt for new acquisitions.

He delighted in extended trips abroad, where his collector's eye might light on anything from ancient Greek vases and oriental rugs to massive stone fireplaces. He never tired of these overseas holidays, pleased to foot the bill for fellow travelers who shared his enthusiasm for cathedrals, art galleries, antique stores, and similar manifestations of Hearstian heaven.

Burton Fredericksen, senior curator for research at the J. Paul Getty Museum, writes, "William Randolph Hearst is no longer thought of as a major collector of art works, which is unfortunate because during his lifetime he bought and sold a large number of important objects. Those he kept were for the most part given to public museums, the majority being now in the Los Angeles County Museum of Art." Fredericksen further describes Hearst as "a prodigious collector, of a nature one now calls compulsive. He does not seem to have attempted to build a collection with the best of everything in it, and indeed, he apparently did not often spend very large amounts to get what he wanted. He bought what he liked and one can assume that he also intended to live with most of what he purchased, though it often, through lack of space, never left the packing crate once he got it."

W. R. Hearst envisioned his San Simeon estate as a showcase for his varied collection, stating as early as 1927, "I see no reason why the ranch should not be a museum of the best things that I can secure." Asked in a 1946 interview about the motivation behind his art purchases, Hearst replied: "I think it is important to have art objects . . . brought to this country. They find their way to museums eventually, and not everybody can go abroad." Even when he was not in residence at San Simeon, historian Robert Pavlik points out, "Hearst, in keeping with his commitment to encourage culture in California, allowed local residents, college students, and members of the Armed Forces to stroll the grounds and gaze upon his art collection and the structures built to house it."

Even though Hearst purchased much of his vast art collection "without much professional help," according to Burton Fredericksen, the collections at San Simeon of antiquities, textiles, paintings, books and manuscripts, nineteenth-century sculpture, and ceilings reveal his expertise.

Two putti, or cherub-like figures, pose temporarily against a backdrop of utilitarian sandbags after uncrating at San Simeon's warehouse. Julia Morgan incorporated a multitude of art pieces and architectural elements into the estate at San Simeon.

The four statues of Sekhmet, the lion-faced Egyptian goddess of war and battle, above, are the oldest works of art at San Simeon, dating from 1350-1200 B.C. Julia Morgan's colored pencil sketch, right, of the setting she envisioned for Sekhmet included Egyptian-inspired tile risers.

Antiquities

Antiquities and classical subjects abound in virtually every medium at San Simeon. The most splendid collection at San Simeon is the Greek vases, which range from the early eighth century to the end of the fourth century B.C., and illustrate Greek figure painting at its finest. Metropolitan Museum of Art curator Dietrich von Bothmer notes that Greek vases were "prized from the moment they left the kiln," and praises eighty pieces the Metropolitan purchased from W. R. Hearst's estate. Hearst's interest in Greek vases was kindled in 1901 by his mother Phoebe. For the next fifty years Hearst added to this collection, making most of his purchases in the 1920s and 1930s. There are 155 vases remaining in the Main Library of La Casa Grande.

Art historians also commend the nine Classical sarcophagi found in the gardens at the Castle. The sarcophagus was used by the Romans as a coffin for above ground interment. Most sarcophagi were made of marble or limestone and adorned with elaborate carving and inscriptions. Perhaps the finest example at San Simeon, a third-century Roman marble sarcophagus depicting the deceased as Apollo accompanied by the Nine Muses, is located on the esplanade near La Casa del Monte.

Textiles

San Simeon is endowed with a magnificent collection of textiles, which Hearst and Morgan used to lavish effect. Textiles found on the hill include tapestries, religious banners and vestments, lace, and oriental rugs—all used throughout the main building and guest houses as wall hangings, floor coverings, and decorative pieces.

The imposing Refectory, where Hearst and his guests dined, is dominated by Palio banners suspended from staffs

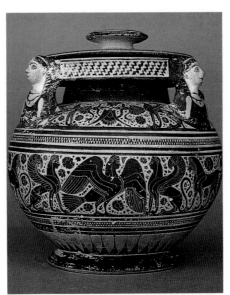

A third-century Roman marble sarcophagus, located on the esplanade near La Casa del Monte, depicts the deceased as Apollo accompanied by the Nine Muses (Polyhymnia, Terpsichore, Thalia, Melpomene, Euterpe, Clio, Erato, Urania, and Calliope) and Athena. Detail, above.

Dating from about 600 B.C., a black-figured Corinthian pyxis, or round box with lid, left, is displayed in the Main Library.

high above the room. Brightly colored silk racing banners like these have been used since the thirteenth century at the biannual Palio Festival in Siena, Italy. The Palio banners in the San Simeon collection date to the eighteenth century, but are now too fragile for permanent display. The originals were removed for conservation and replaced with painstakingly-made reproductions.

Perhaps the most notable of San Simeon's many textiles is the *mille fleurs* (literally "thousands of flowers") tapestry hanging in the Billiard Room. Tapestries such as these derive their name from the

The seventeenth-century wool tapestry, above, depicts the shield of the Spanish viceroy to Peru, one of several examples of armorial tapestries on the hilltop.

Hearst's textile collection includes oriental rugs, religious vestments, and intricately worked pieces such as an Italian table cover with the crest of the Gonzaga family, below right, handcrafted using silk thread.

carpet of flowers in the background. Woven of wool and silk, the tapestry depicts a stag hunt and was probably completed about 1500 in Flanders. It is considered to be one of only "a handful of *mille fleurs* tapestries from this period in the entire world." Hearst acquired the tapestry in 1928 from art dealer Joseph Duveen.

The tapestries on view in the massive Assembly Room illustrate an elaborate style dating from the mid-sixteenth century. Four woven panels, each measuring over 300 square feet, depict the struggles of Roman general Scipio Africanus during the Punic Wars. The rare wool and silk Flemish tapestries, made in about 1550 from drawings by Italian artist Giulio Romano, were inspired by the Latin epic poem *Africa*. As Hearst himself explained to frequent guest Adela Rogers St. Johns, "A tapestry can contain many scenes, many people, many combinations . . . but they all exist together, simultaneously, and that is the joy of the tapestry." Huge tapestries such as these served a functional as well as decorative purpose, for they improved acoustics and prevented drafts in medieval stone rooms. To determine the height of the Assemby Room, Julia

Morgan added the height of the Flemish tapestries to the choir stalls Hearst wished to use as wainscoting.

Morgan initiated a spraying system to protect the textiles from moths. For restoration work, she used greenhouse worker Alfredo Gomes and another Portuguese employee, who "sat right flat on their fannies on top of the pool table or whatever was available for them, and sewed and sewed and sewed and sewed, month after month," recalled construction supervisor George Loorz, "and I'll tell you that it was difficult to tell where they started and where they [left] off. They did an excellent job."

William Randolph Hearst inherited a number of the oriental carpets now at San Simeon from his mother, Phoebe Apperson Hearst, and supplemented them with his own purchases. Over a hundred rugs remain on the hilltop, most dating from the last decades of the nineteenth century. Many traditional styles are represented, including carpets from the Persian regions Kerman, Tabriz, Meshed, Kazak, Bakhtiari, and Heriz, as well as China. Hand-knotted in silk, cotton, wool, or camel hair, these rugs represent thousands of hours of creative work by skilled artisans.

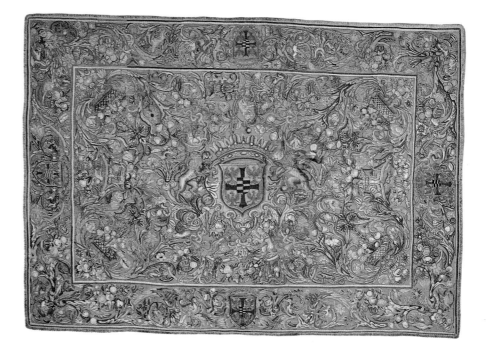

Simon Vouet (1590-1649) painted this seventeenth-century French oil, entitled Neptune and Amphitrite. The painting, and its companion, Diana and Endymion, were installed as ceiling panels in the lower south duplex.

German artist Franz Xavier Winterhalter painted the portrait of Carlotta, Empress of Mexico, above, in 1864. Along with its companion portrait of Emperor Maximilian, the painting hangs in a guestroom in La Casa del Mar.

The sixeenth-century Florentine polychrome stucco bas-relief Madonna and Child, above right, after Antonio Rossellino, graces a wall of the gilded lower lobby of La Casa del Mar.

Enamel plaques, each depicting a scene from the mythological life of Hercules, by French artist Jean de Court of Limoges enhance the sixteenth-century cabinet, right, displayed in the Billiard Room.

The sitting room of the Celestial Suite in La Casa Grande is the location of French artist Luc Olivier-Merson's 1879 painting Rest on the Flight into Egypt, opposite, top, which Hearst bought in 1894.

Guests in the lower south duplex saw this ceiling painting, opposite, lower left, over the bed before they closed their eyes at night. Simon Vouet's Diana and Endymion tells the story of Endymion, who achieved immortal youth and beauty through eternal sleep. He was visited each night in the cave where he slept by the goddess Selene.

Hearst purchased Madonna and Child *by the Flemish painter Adrian Isenbrandt, above, in 1928; it hangs in the sittingroom of La Casa del Mar.*

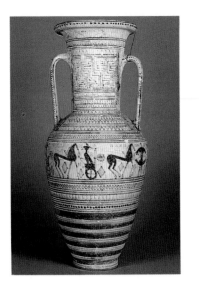

The Baring amphora, above, dates to the eighth century B.C., and is the oldest of 155 Greek vases remaining at San Simeon.

Julia Morgan designed the library on the second floor of La Casa Grande, right, to house a portion of Hearst's vast book collection where guests could see it. His splendid collection of Greek vases is displayed in this room. Each piece is fixed in place for protection in the event of earthquakes.

When at his San Simeon estate, W. R. Hearst conducted business from his private enclave, the third-floor Gothic Library, opposite. His libraries were kept behind locked iron grilles, far right, designed by Morgan. Guests were able to examine Hearst's books on request.

Books and Manuscripts

The second floor library of La Casa Grande holds 4,102 volumes; another 3,736 volumes are present in the Gothic Library. These figures represent only a fraction of Hearst's books, manuscripts, and autographs, most of which were sold at several Parke-Bernet auctions in November of 1938 or at Gimbels in 1941, after Hearst experienced a major financial crisis. In addition to the visible shelf space in the Gothic Library, Morgan designed locked cabinets and two hidden book vaults, which tripled the storage capacity. Planning for the libraries began in August of 1929 when Hearst wrote to Morgan:

> *Enclosed is a list of books belonging to my mother which are stored. I do not like to have books stored. They go to pieces. I think we should arrange in some way to have library shelves at San Simeon for these books. . . . Perhaps the best plan would be to make spacious*

> *book-cases in the new Gothic room that we intend to make by raising the roof of the main building.*

Hearst's libraries were kept behind locked iron grilles designed by Morgan. Guests could examine these books on request, or choose a bestseller that they could take to their room from a separate lending library.

The 1938 auction catalogues described Hearst as having "an intuitive sense" for collecting letters and documents relating to history, biography, and literature. His "ever-increasing purpose to have each item represent some famous event" was well-satisfied in his vast collections. The earliest American piece was a 1638 Native American deed for Exeter, New Hampshire. The largest collection related to the Revolutionary War, with most of the signers of the Declaration of Independence represented, including a rare autograph of Georgia legislator Button Gwinnett.

Hearst also assembled a fine collection of depositions and jurors' accounts from the witchcraft trials of Salem, Massachusetts.

The first newspaper printed in California (from Monterey in 1847) was a prized possession of the publisher's, supplemented by several other scarce California newspapers from this period. He also had materials relating to San Francisco's Committee of Vigilance, one of the primary examples of frontier justice in American history.

Hearst also collected books and manuscripts from abroad, such as an Egyptian papyrus manuscript of *The Book of the Dead*, circa 600 B.C.; dozens of illuminated manuscripts from thirteenth-century Flanders and sixteenth-century France, Italy, and Spain; a 1561 edition of *The Works of Geoffrey Chaucer*; a rare medieval French and Latin document signed, "Catherine de Medici, Queen of France"; and Marie Antoinette's own four-volume set of the 1769 imprint *Discours sur la Nature les Dogmes de la Religion Gauloise*, signed by her and stamped with her coat of arms in 24-carat gold on the binding.

The largest literary collection, by far, related to Charles Dickens, Hearst's favorite author. After the choicest pieces were sold at auction in 1938, Hearst still had eighteen signed letters; sixteen first editions with original sketches from George Cruikshank and Hablot Knight Browne; nineteen family letters; fifty-two examples of Dickensiana; and twenty-four limited edition, finely bound sets of Dickens' complete works.

The hilltop libraries today still house most of Hearst's exhaustive collections on art, architecture, travel, landscaping and gardening, and British literature. The publisher's library has signed presentation copies of novels or autobiographies by Edna Ferber, Somerset Maugham, H. G. Wells, James Hilton, Faith Baldwin, and others who contributed pieces to his magazines or visited San Simeon.

Hearst also collected letters, documents, and books of United States presidents George Washington, Abraham Lincoln, Thomas Jefferson, John Adams, Andrew Jackson, Ulysses S. Grant, William McKinley, Warren Harding, Benjamin Harrison, Andrew Johnson, and Zachary Taylor. He owned Thomas Jefferson's Bible and ten other volumes from his library at Monticello, together with Jefferson's own draft of an 1806 address to Osage and Sioux Native American leaders, and letters about his slaves. Hearst gathered twenty-eight letters and documents from George Washington's boyhood to his death in 1799, including letters about his plans for Mount Vernon, freedom of the press, and his presidency; he collected twenty-five books once owned by George Washington, including the eight-volume 1776 imprint of Thomas Simmes' *Military Guide for Young Officers*, with Washington's signature on the flyleaf. The most important letter in the collection was written by Washington at Valley Forge in 1778. Lincoln materials were equally plentiful: handwritten stays of execution for Union soldiers who had deserted; directives to his generals; letters to his wife Mary Todd; a signed copy of one of the very few books Lincoln owned as a boy; and a twenty-four-volume collection of Lincoln's complete works with twenty-five original Lincoln documents as the final volume. He also owned an original broadside playbill from Ford's Theatre for the performance on the night of Lincoln's assassination.

Sculpture

Two of San Simeon's finest statues, each executed in the highly Romantic style of the late nineteenth century, are found in the vestibule of the main building. On the south is *Bacchante*, a marble rendering of a work in bronze by American sculptor Frederick MacMonnies, who had a studio in Paris. The bronze sculpture, a dancing female nude with a baby in one hand and grapes held high in the other, was offered to the Boston Public Library by its original owner, architect Charles McKim. Boston's leading citizens protested the donation, arguing that the "work was improper for a building with intellectual purpose," because it glorified drunkenness, illegitimate motherhood, nudity, and a host of other immoralities. Hearst inherited MacMonnies' marble version of the sculpture from his mother.

On the left of the vestibule is Jean-Léon Gérôme's *Pygmalion and Galatea*, another example of the Romantic style of the late Victorian period. The graceful rendering of the two figures is accomplished in white marble faintly tinted with paint. The theme of the sculpture is well known: the sculptor Pygmalion creates a female statue so beautiful he is unable to resist falling in love with it. Venus answers his prayers and brings the statue to life. Another sculpture by Gérôme at San Simeon, the bronze group *Anacreon*, is located in one of the duplex rooms in the main building.

A second statue of Galatea is located on the main terrace ornamental pool in front of La Casa Grande. Hearst inherited *Galatea on a Dolphin* by Leopoldo Ansiglioni from his mother, Phoebe, who had been a benefactor of the sculptor. In 1889, after visiting Ansiglioni's workshop, W. R. wrote to Phoebe:

> *Why didn't you buy Ansiglioni's Galatea. It is superb. . . . I have a great notion to buy it myself, in fact, the one thing that prevents me is a scarcity of funds as it were. The man wants eight thousand dollars for the blooming thing and that is a little above my head. I have the art fever terribly. Queer, isn't it? I never miss a gallery now and I go and mosey about the pictures and statuary and admire them and wish they were mine.*

W. R. Hearst had the sculpture shipped to San Simeon in 1922 from his mother's estate and placed it on the main terrace in the mid-1920s.

Sculpture from Hearst's collection at San Simeon includes a ceramic bust of a Florentine nobleman, top; *Frederick MacMonnies' marble* Bacchante, above; *and the Ansiglioni* Galatea, below, *displayed on the main terrace opposite the entrance to La Casa Grande.*

The marble Venus, opposite, *is by Antonio Canova.*

The sitting room of La Casa del Mar features an armorial ceiling pendant, above. Crafted from gilded wood, it depicts the coat of arms and mitre of a sixteenth-century Spanish bishop.

W. R. Hearst's bedroom, right, on the third floor of La Casa Grande is surprisingly modest, decorated with photographs and paintings of sentimental value—including pictures of his parents and maternal grandparents. A matchless fourteenth-century Spanish ceiling completes the room.

A Gothic ceiling, made in northern Spain in the fifteenth century, dominates the Billiard Room, opposite. The table at the north end of the room was used when playing the game of pocket billiards, or pool. The second table was used for billiards, a game of skill involving three balls.

Ceilings

Rare antique ceilings are evident throughout the houses at San Simeon, often supplemented by wood or plaster reproductions made by Morgan's crafts workers. George Loorz, who supervised the installation of most of the exceptional ceilings at San Simeon, remembered, "Most of the time the ceilings did not have enough original material. In a few instances we had too much left over, but [Hearst had] too much pride . . . to duplicate and have the same ceiling in another room." Most of the historic ceilings are Spanish, acquired for Hearst by Arthur and Mildred Stapley Byne, art dealers who were once curators at the Hispanic Society of America in New York.

The painted pine ceiling with exposed beams that graces the Billiard Room is an excellent example of the artisans' craft from northern Spain. It was offered to Hearst by Arthur Byne in 1930. Byne wrote to recommend the purchase,

noting that the ceiling "is a very important fifteenth-century example, Gothic in period and style and similar to the one recently put up in the Metropolitan Museum, New York. This ceiling is decorated in the best tradition of the Spanish ceiling painters, with the Moorish triangles formed of little white lozenges framing heraldic scenes. If you are not interested in it, I shall probably send it on to the Boston Museum." Hearst, of course, could not resist—the ceiling came to San Simeon.

Morgan installed a choice fourteenth-century Spanish ceiling in Hearst's Gothic Suite bedroom. Exceedingly rare, the ceiling had long been separated from its frieze panels. Arthur Byne first found the ceiling in a house in the town of Tereul; he then found the original frieze panels in an aristocrat's house in Aragon. Byne reunited the elements and offered the rare ceiling to Hearst, who had it shipped to San Simeon in 1924.

Architect Julia Morgan's watercolor for a tile design, top, and a sketch of a decorative detail.

Incredibly, there were times when Hearst's mammoth warehouses failed him and it was necessary to make reproductions of the art, furniture, or ornamentation he envisioned for a particular room. Here Morgan also excelled, for she had contacts abroad to locate the artisans who were skilled workers in wood, iron, tile, stone and glass. In some instances artisans had already emigrated to California, as in the case of Jules Suppo, a master woodcarver.

Suppo was born in Switzerland and learned his craft in Paris. He met Morgan in 1915 when he arrived in San Francisco to work on buildings for the Panama-Pacific International Exposition. George Loorz remembered the artisan as "quite eccentric, but very talented." In 1923 Morgan called on Suppo to add "huge carvings up underneath the eaves of the [main] building," according to Fred Jordan, a woodcarver who worked with Suppo. With the proceeds from his Hearst commissions, Suppo was able to set up his own shop, which Morgan designed for him at 2423 Polk Street in San Francisco. Fred Jordan joined him at the new location, where they worked on "the Hearst job" intermittently from 1923 to 1940.

For the "huge carvings" or friezes around the exterior of La Casa Grande, Morgan ordered Siam teakwood, a soft wood with "a lot of silica and sand in it. And you run it over the joiner or through the saws and the sparks fly. It dulls the machinery very quickly and also the carving tools," Jordan remembered. "But that's what was specified, so they ordered twenty or thirty thousand feet from J. E. Higgins, the lumber company in San Francisco."

A few of the big timbers were secured from a shipyard to begin the work, but the amount needed was so large and the wood so prized that it took five years to complete the order. Jordan explained the delay: "In Siam, the elephants handled all those big timbers, and they float it downstream. Well, if they had two, three dry years, you don't get any timbers. So it took five years." Morgan completed most of the design for the La Casa Grande teakwood friezes, but "later on she left a lot up to Suppo and he was very clever. . . . He was a little bit of a short man, but he was a good artist," recalled Jordan.

Morgan came to Suppo's San Francisco shop on occasion, where Jordan had the opportunity to meet and work with her. Jordan remembers Morgan as "very brilliant. . . . She could recall [decorative] details that we'd made five or six years ago. . . . She'd sketch it out and she recalled. What a memory she had. She was a very remarkable woman."

In addition to the work Suppo and Jordan completed in San Francisco, construction superintendent George Loorz recalled, "I had one or two [workers at San Simeon] all the time carving wood . . . small figures that went on doorknobs and cornices and caps." Skilled carpenters and joiners also worked out of the hilltop woodshop, which was located across the road from the Roman Pool. Byron Hanchett, a San Simeon employee and careful observer of the scene, recalls:

> During 1946 the shop was busy turning out work for the new wing under construction. The outside of the shop looked like an old lumber shack, but upon entering, one wished for a guide to explain all the tools and activities. The workmen never looked up from their work, as they were accustomed to frequent visitors.
>
> Odd-shaped wooden moldings, carved faces, fancy doors, and extra pieces of carved wood hung from the ceiling beams and walls. Some of the tools were handmade to do special jobs. On the workbenches, planes with jagged blades, chisels with cupped edges, square nails, old hinges, and large wood clamps were scattered about. The cabinet

drawers were full of modern and antique hardware.

Many of the workers were skilled at fancy woodwork. Some carved work to replace damaged pieces. They duplicated these old pieces to the extent of even drilling worm holes. Different sizes of chain were used to beat the wood to age it, since different chains left different marks. After the painter finished his work, only a skilled crafts-man could tell the difference between the old and the new.

Dutch artisan John Van der Loo and his father, Theo, ran the cast stone shop at San Simeon. Skilled in the art of crafting or reproducing art objects and architectural elements, the Van der Loos were prodigious workers. They used white concrete and fine white sand for a superior grade of concrete, which was poured into plaster or glue molds to make balustrades, railings, coping, lamp standards, and limestone "surrounds."

The Van der Loos were favorites of Morgan's because they produced pieces of consistent and remarkable quality.

"An awful lot of it was done where we did the same thing over and over," according to George Loorz, such as the two-foot-high "little lions," as Hearst called them. These *sejant-erect* cast stone animals bearing shields are San Simeon's hallmark, the first art objects visitors to the hilltop usually see. John Van der Loo completed a great deal of cast stone interior trim for fireplaces, windows, and doorways and made the cast plaster caryatids in the movie theater. At Morgan's request he also produced three-dimensional cast plaster models of carving designs so that she and Hearst could judge the effect before the work was accomplished.

The Spanish and Mediterranean architectural styles that Hearst favored for San Simeon relied on a great deal of ornamental ironwork. Morgan used Ed Trinkkeller of Los Angeles, who had

Artisans skilled in wood, stone, and iron were vital to the process of creating San Simeon. Light streams through the windows of master woodcarver Jules Suppo's workshop, left, on Polk Street in San Francisco. Top, John Van der Loo (posing on the right with his handiwork), was skilled in the art of casting stone and plaster. Above, a detail of the gilded wrought iron door grilles crafted by German ironworker Ed Trinkkeller for the entrance of La Casa del Sol. Made in 1924, the grilles feature multiple profiles, each unique.

San Simeon's outdoor Neptune Pool, flanked by colonnades and a Greek temple façade, is perhaps the most superb of the many outdoor pools designed by architect Julia Morgan during her long career. The Neptune Pool holds 345,000 gallons of water. The basin of the pool is white marble; refraction of light makes the water appear blue.

worked on the Los Angeles *Examiner* building in 1915; he was especially gifted in reproducing ironwork Hearst had in his collections. Morgan had strict ideas about how the iron should be aged to simulate an antique patina, using rottenstone (a siliceous limestone decomposed to a friable state, used for polishing metals) and oil. George Loorz remembered:

> *That was our dust. Then you rubbed as much as you wanted. You couldn't rub too much because you wanted to leave some show. And she [Morgan] preferred me not to put mechanics on that. She thought that to give it that same effect, that laborers could do it better because that's the way the antiques came. They were done by unskilled laborers in the monasteries and so forth, in Europe. So she said it was a lack of artistic ability*

to have these good guys on it, made it too good. . . . She was pretty clever.

The Neptune Pool, perhaps the most splendid outdoor pool Morgan ever designed, required artisans skilled in marble and cast stone and took twelve years to perfect. Hearst had first asked for a landscaped garden with a small ornamental lily pond, which he referred to as the Temple Garden. On March 31, 1924, as another of construction supervisor C. C. Rossi's crews began to excavate the site, Hearst wrote:

> *I am sending back the plan of the temple garden with the suggestion that we make the pool longer than it is . . . and that we make it eight feet deep so that we can use it as a swimming pool. Mrs. Hearst and the children are extremely anxious to*

The Neptune Pool took twelve years to perfect, beginning in 1924. The statuary awaiting permanent placement (left) is the work of Charles-Georges Cassou, who carved the marble groups in Paris and shipped them to San Simeon in 1930. Hearst's financial reverses in the late 1930s prevented additional acquisitions from Cassou. Some statues commissioned by Hearst eventually made their way to Forest Lawn Memorial Park in Glendale, California.

Above, household staff members Emma and Hilda Christensen pose on the poolside terrace in the 1930s.

have a swimming pool, and unwilling to wait until we can get the regular swimming pools built. . . . Therefore, if it seems practicable, please make this a swimming pool—temporarily at least.

Morgan converted the design to a pool that would fit the site. By July of 1924 it was ready for the family's use. Two years later Hearst requested a much larger pool with a cascade and more statuary. Morgan designed the changes, and Rossi's crews began jackhammering the "old" pool. Construction on the enlargement lasted for two years. The pool crew was supervised by Frank "Babe" Souza, the toughest labor boss on the hilltop. Guido Minetti, who worked on various jobs for six years at San Simeon, labored for a short time under Souza on the Neptune Pool, pushing "cement buggies," or wheelbarrows filled with fresh concrete. "I only weighed about 104 pounds, and the first buggy I dropped. I spilled cement all over . . . , so then he took me off and I was dumping [cement] sacks into the mixer, and we were using four sacks to each

mixer." Minetti soon transferred to the position of "bull cook" supervising the Chinese cooks and mess hall.

The Vermont Marble Company of Proctor, Vermont, quarried the marble used for the second pool. Louis Saylor, a Vermont Marble employee, worked at San Simeon for several months on the project. As he was completing the job in 1928, Morgan and Hearst asked for estimates of the cost of a colonnade, or series of solid marble columns, to bracket the pool. Vermont Marble then quarried and shipped the marble for the columns as a rush order at Hearst's personal request.

In 1934 Hearst asked Morgan to expand the pool once again to accommodate the present Greek temple facade, a larger cascade, additional statue-filled alcoves, and the long-contemplated colonnade. About this time Louis Saylor unexpectedly met Julia Morgan in San Francisco, where she told him they had only just uncrated the "rush order" marble columns.

The third and final incarnation of the Neptune Pool holds 345,000 gallons

Reflecting light above and below the water, the tiles of the Roman Pool, above, are made of gold leaf fused with Venetian glass. The marble pool ladders were designed by Morgan.

Dozens of drawings for the indoor pool, right, were made by Camille Solon, a French-English painter who worked for several years to perfect the pool's mosaics.

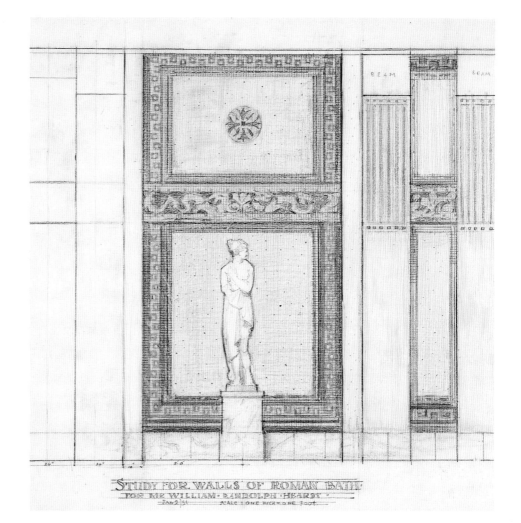

STUDY FOR WALLS OF ROMAN BATH
FOR MR WILLIAM · RANDOLPH · HEARST
JAN 2 '31   SCALE 1 ONE INCH = ONE FOOT

of water in a 104-foot-long white marble-lined basin. Morgan also designed the pool's filters, made of beach sand and located under the western colonnade. At the time, oil-burning boilers, located in a small separate building, heated the pool. Seventeen art deco-lettered dressing rooms, with spare suits and caps for forgetful guests, line the upper terrace south of the pool.

Artisans were also vital to the construction of the Roman Pool, a remarkable indoor swimming pool lined with mosaics of tile made from 22-carat hammered gold and delicate Venetian glass, which took seven years to complete. Although Hearst's initial instructions called for marble walls and the glass tiles for the basin of the pool, eventually the plans were enlarged to cover every surface of the interior, including the walls and ceiling, with the deep blue and gold mosaics.

Hearst contemplated a salt water pool as early as 1922 but could not decide whether to place it near his favorite picnic grounds on San Simeon Point or on the hilltop. In 1925 he was still deliberating, wiring Morgan on May 14 from New York:

EXPECT TO BE WEST LAST OF THIS MONTH . . . HOW FAR ARE VARIOUS PROJECTS INSIDE AND OUTSIDE ADVANCED HOW ABOUT TENNIS COURT THIS IS IMPORTANT HOW ABOUT MAIN ENTRANCE TO EAST HOW ABOUT ASSEMBLY ROOM AND DINING ROOM DO WE NEED ANY RUGS IF ANYTHING IS TO BE GOTTEN HERE LET ME KNOW BEFORE I LEAVE 2 WOULD LIKE SALT WATER SWIMMING POOL WILL MACHINERY WHICH USED TO RUN

By the end of the month, Morgan
and Hearst had decided that the existing
tennis courts on the north end of the
estate would be demolished and replaced
with an indoor fresh-water pool, dressing
and rest rooms, exercise room, Turkish
bath, and handball and squash courts.
Two tennis courts would be restored to
the same location, but this time they
would be on the roof of the indoor
pool building.

According to tile artisan Joseph
Giarritta, the idea for the glass tile
mosaics for the Roman Pool came from
Morgan, who had seen a similar pool
in Venice, Italy. Others attribute it to
Hearst, who admired Ravenna's Mauso-
leum of Galla Placidia, with its arches of
blue and gold glass tiles. The one-inch-
square tiles, produced using a very old
technique known as *smalti*, are made of
three layers of fired glass, gold foil, and
ordinary glass. Cobalt oxide was introduced into the glass of some of the tiles
to produce the deep blue color. To
produce the mosaic effect, tiles with
gradations of colors were made. The
tiles for the Roman Pool were produced
on Murano, an island near Venice
famous for its glassmaking.

Camille Solon, an French-English
painter who worked for several years
at San Simeon on the Celestial Suite
and the Gothic Library, was asked by
Morgan to work on the indoor pool.
He designed the patterns for the
mosaics, which were laboriously transferred to hand-ruled graph paper by
Solon and members of Morgan's staff.
On September 21, 1932, Hearst protested using Solon, writing:

*Mr. Solon is wonderful as a designer
and a colorist, but slows up the work*
*tremendously by continual changes in
the scheme and program. . . . Let us get
a set and satisfactory design and color
scheme, and then put in artistic workmen
to carry it out. Mr. Solon will be
valuable if he does not interfere. If he
does, would suggest, Miss Morgan, that
you find need for him in San Francisco.
I would like to see the pool ready on the
date promised. I'm sure it will not be
ready unless we proceed in a more
practical manner.*

Morgan stood by the artist, who
completed the design on time and then
worked closely with the Italian tile
artisans on the difficult job of hand-
setting the one-inch tiles to the pattern.
Florence-born John Pellegrini, who
placed the third-century Roman marble
mosaic in the vestibule of La Casa
Grande, directed this task. He rented a
large warehouse in San Francisco where
the Roman Pool mosaic cutting tables
and storage were set up. "Mr. Hearst
wanted to give this job to a firm in
Venice," remembered Pellegrini, but
"Miss Morgan said, 'Why give it to
Venice? You always feature "Buy American" [in Hearst newspapers]. You might
as well give it to someone here.' "

For two years, Pellegrini worked
with Nino Falsieri and Primo Caredio at
the Green Street warehouse, completing
four-foot sections of mosaic at a time
with Solon's help and weekly visits
from Morgan. Of this process, Joseph
Giarritta recalled:

*All the men that worked on the cutting
of the mosaic and putting it on paper
were all experts in their fields. All were
of Italian descent. The mosaic cutters
worked on these long tables with the
designs in front of them. They would cut
different colored mosaics to match the
colors that Mr. Solon put on the designs.
They put a little glue on each stone and
pasted it on the design. This kind of
work is done by experts and is exacting
and tiresome. Mr. Solon checked the
designs when they were finished. He was*

*In April of 1927 Hearst contemplated
adding salt water to the expanded Neptune
Pool; in the same letter a second pool
occurred to him, as he wrote to Morgan:*

I have an idea for a winter pool.
We could put a big hot-house
down where we were going to
build the Persian garden, and in
the middle of this hot-house we
could have a big pool about the
size of our present pool. In the
hot-house, sufficiently back from
the pool, we would have palms,
ferns and a whole lot of orchids.
In fact, it would be mainly an
orchid hot-house. . . . The
temperature of the hot-house,
and of the pool, too, would be
warm on the coldest, bleakest
winter day.

<u>We would have the South Sea
Islands on the Hill</u>. . . . We could
have latticed windows as in that
picture of the harem that we were
looking at when discussing the
Turkish bath. Towards the sea
there should be a big rest room,
and a loggia. . . . The pool,
of course, would be the main
attraction; and we might put a
turtle and a couple of sharks in
to lend versimilitude [sic].

This, except for the sharks, is
not as impractical a proposition
as it might seem. It is merely
making a hot-house useful,
and making a pool beautiful.

Morgan responded on May 2, writing:

I like your idea for the
combination indoor pool and
orchid green house. It should
be very tropical and exotic.
There could be a plate glass
partition in the pool and the
alligators, sharks, etc. could
disport themselves on one side
of it and visitors could
unsuspectingly dive toward it.
(This is the other architect's
[i.e., Morgan's] contribution
to your idea.)

A detailed view of the blue and gold mosaics of the Roman Pool, above. Classical marble statues, right, are placed around the pool.

a wonderful person, knew just what he wanted, and how it would look when it was finished. When the designs were finished, they were set aside to dry. These men were in their late years, and I do not believe that there are any more like them around.

Giarritta's knowledge of marble and mosaics came from his father and uncles who had arrived in San Francisco from Italy in 1904; he inherited the supervision of the tile installation at the Roman Pool when his uncle fell ill. As Pellegrini completed sections of mosaic in San Francisco, they were sent to San Simeon, where Giarritta "installed the mosaic according to the [blue]prints, in the exact location where Miss Morgan wanted it. There was no margin for error for Miss Morgan. . . . No thing escaped her eyes." Giarritta continued:

When I first started setting the mosaic, I had a section up, the mortar was still soft. Miss Morgan said it looked too perfect, and she wanted us to try to figure a way to make it look older but still look perfect. I suggested I bang my fist in it in different parts of the panel, change the smooth face of the mosaic with the small depressions, here and there. She said try it. I did, and she said that's just what she wanted. I continued that procedure all along until we finished the pool.

The most difficult part of the Roman Pool mosaic installation was on the ceiling beams, where the tilesetters were compelled to work upside down. Of the pool itself, Giarritta commented, "The gutters are set so perfectly that the water goes over the gutters at the exact same time, all over the pool," creating a mirror effect on the the ripple-free water.

The pool, dressing rooms, and the tennis courts were the only features of the elaborate "Tennis-Gymnasium Building" to be finished. The rooftop courts never drained properly, causing water damage to the pool below despite repeated attempts over the years to solve the problem. Additional damage occurred when Hearst decided that he still wanted a salt water pool. Against his architect's and plumber's advice, eighteen tons of salt were hauled up the hill and added to the pool's water. Despite three years of tinkering, the salt water effect was unremarkable to guests and damaging to the plumbing and hammered gold in the tiles. The plumbing was repaired and fresh water reintroduced, but use of the pool was infrequent, despite its beauty, because the heated water created a sauna-like atmosphere that guests found uncomfortable. Although Hearst intended the pool primarily for night-time use, evenings were usually taken up with the ritual film screening, which further reduced the use of this pool.

In addition to the artisans, gardeners, and construction laborers, Hearst's estate also required versatile workers to maintain the electrical, water, and plumbing systems; cowboys to tend the ranch's horses and cattle; office staff for bookkeeping and payrolls; operators for the switchboard, shortwave radio, teletype, and telegraph; and workers for the dairy, vegetable garden, poultry ranch, zoo and dog kennels, stables, estate security, and the airstrip and hangar at the bottom of the hill.

Hearst was fortunate to find Marks Harry Eubanks, an electrician and native of Cambria who gradually assumed responsibility for all the maintenance functions. Eubanks started working on the estate in 1919 when he returned from World War I and remained until his death in 1952. Although he assisted with construction from time to time, Eubanks

was primarily responsible for maintaining power, water, and phone systems. He also served as fire chief; all San Simeon workers assisted with fire prevention.

Byron Hanchett, who worked for Eubanks, recalls the electrician's deep affection for San Simeon, which he considered "a second home." Eubanks, head gardener Nigel Keep, construction superintendent George Loorz, and their families lived next to each other in charming Morgan-designed, Spanish-tiled stucco houses on the bay in the village of San Simeon. Don Pancho Estrada, descendent of the family who held the original Mexican land grants for San Simeon, lived in the house closest to the warehouses. Estrada's son-in-law, Roy Sommers, served as wharfinger for San Simeon.

Perhaps the most challenging of the many aspects of Eubanks' job was keeping power and phone lines up during stormy winter nights. He would often have to saddle a horse and "ride the line" until he located the downed line. Cold and wet, he would climb the pole and work, often on high-voltage lines, alone in the dark, all the while watching for field animals from the zoo. Sherman Eubanks, Marks' son, recalls, "When a party was here, or when Mr. Hearst and Marion were here, he would be [on the hilltop] twenty-four hours a day. And one of the things that always bothered him was that they used to have to take the elevator down to the Assembly Room. And once in a while the power would go out, and Mr. Hearst would get stuck in the elevator. Those were kind of touchy times."

Coal oil lanterns were used for light during the early phases of construction, until the powerhouse was built and a gasoline generator installed in 1921. Morgan devised a generator and a waterwheel on a stream about fifty yards from the powerhouse as a backup system, to which the electrical load was switched every night at midnight. In 1928 the first power lines were brought to the ranch,

Marks Eubanks, electrician and maintenance supervisor for the San Simeon estate, describes his responsibilities: "In doing my work around here, I try to keep a low profile. I don't work where guests are assembled. If something breaks down, it must be made to work, one way or another, until Mr. Hearst and his guests leave. Then it can be repaired properly. I feel Mr. Hearst has enough on his mind without worrying about some breakdown."

Hearst was often called away from social gatherings at San Simeon for urgent communications—his extensive business empire operated around the clock. One of Hearst's newspaper employees, R. L. Burgess, felt that he and other reporters "were like doormen, huntsmen, footmen, male nurses, during my five years on the Hearst newspapers. We were incessantly running errands for the absentee nabob: like most of his employees, I never saw the great man in the flesh." Burgess concluded, "The old boy with all his faults was a downright American individualist at heart."

A sunny nook in the southeast corner of the Billiard Room, right, features a spandrel of seventeenth-century polychrome tiles illustrating the Persian poem, Shah Nama.

the village, and the hilltop by Midland Counties Public Service Association, the local electric utility. In 1947 Pacific Gas & Electric improved service when all original lines were replaced.

Hazel Eubanks taught five children in the village schoolhouse, including her son, Sherman, and for a time, Hearst's grandson, John Hearst, Jr. She came from Astoria, Oregon, in 1920 to teach school in Cambria where she met her future husband. Of Hearst she remembered, "*Life* magazine was a rival publication, and Mr. Hearst refused to subscribe to it, but he did like to read it. So I would send him my copy every week, which he appreciated. In return, he had a year's worth of issues of [Hearst publications] *Good Housekeeping* and *Cosmopolitan* bound in volumes and instructed [his secretary] Col. Willicombe to send them to me."

Joseph Willicombe directed the San

Simeon staff who maintained Hearst's contact with the outside world. The switchboard at San Simeon, located in a separate building near the construction camp, was staffed twenty-four hours a day, using local women, such as Eileen Rohrberg, who had worked for the phone company in Cambria. They were often supplemented with operators from the Los Angeles *Examiner*, who were skilled in the art of placing Hearst's many long-distance calls, a complex proposition in the days before direct long-distance dialing. There was no telephone number as such for the Hearst estate, which was known simply as "Hacienda" to operators far and wide.

Extension phones were also a rarity in the 1920s, but Hearst had eighty phones installed all over the hilltop, including the swimming pools, tennis courts, and terraces. The village and ranch had an additional thirty-six phones that linked the cowboy camps of the ranch all the way to Jolon, thirty rugged brush-and-rattlesnake-filled miles distant from San Simeon. Marks Eubanks' crew was responsible for installing and maintaining the line, but the cowboys kept a trail cleared so the electricians could reach it. Byron Hanchett, who worked on the phone line in the 1940s, recalls Hearst's fondness for riding overland to Jolon and picnicking with a party of guests. On occasion, Hearst would call about a week ahead to let Eubanks know where he would like additional phones placed. *Fortune* magazine reported the story, perhaps apocryphal, of

> the executive who fell to wondering how
> a ball game came out while seated by a
> camp fire with Mr. Hearst, a day's ride
> from the castle. "I'll tell you," volunteers
> Mr. Hearst and, fumbling with the rock
> against which he was leaning, pulls from
> there a telephone, asks for New York,
> and relieves his guest's curiosity.

This seventeenth-century canopy bed was used by Hearst during the time he occupied La Casa del Mar.

The fourth cloister guest room in La Casa Grande features highly glazed ceramic sculptures from the della Robbia workshops in Italy.

Franklin and Helen Whitcomb, who worked for Hearst's International News Service and the Los Angeles *Examiner* respectively, came regularly to San Simeon to work in the communications office. Bert Acton was a telegraph operator who worked at San Simeon, whose "main job was handling the Morse telegrams to Mr. Hearst, the guests, and sending out anything that they wanted to send out, specifically to a particular editor or individual," recalls Mr. Whitcomb. Acton, and his successor Jack Adams, had a direct line to the Western Union office in San Luis Obispo.

Two teletype machines, one of which was located in the hilltop office and the other at the north end of the Assembly Room in the main building,

were added, along with a shortwave radio that was a favorite pastime of Hearst's oldest son, George. San Simeon staff communicated by prearranged schedule daily with Los Angeles, arranging for supplies and items requested by Hearst to be sent up with the day's newspapers. A newspaper employee left Los Angeles at 3:00 every morning with fresh editions of the *Examiner* and the print of the Hollywood movie to be shown that night in the theatre. The courier arrived at San Simeon at about ten in the morning; the round trip was made daily. Later the trip was made using one of Hearst's three airplanes.

When Hearst was in residence on the hilltop, the tempo also quickened in the nearby village of Cambria and San

Simeon. Zel Bordegary, a Cambria resident who handled laundry for the estate, remembers:

> The whole village of San Simeon . . . all those houses were filled with employees. There were many folks in [Cambria] that worked for Mr. Hearst when he was here and many of them went up to Wyntoon when he went up to Wyntoon. They just went right along with him. There were telephone operators and office clerks and there was a gentleman in charge of the vegetable garden, there was a chicken ranch, there were just all sorts of things going on.

The poultry ranch house that Morgan designed is perhaps one of her finest efforts, similar to the Spanish-influenced houses near San Simeon's wharf. Morgan devised a system for the 1,500 laying hens quite modern for its day, with gently slanted troughs designed to catch eggs as they were laid and collect them in one location. Several varieties of pheasant were raised in addition to chickens for San Simeon's tables.

In 1925 Hearst wrote a lengthy letter to Morgan on the more prosaic parts of the ranch operation. After three pages detailing his wishes for "gardens—flights of steps—cascades—fountains, gates—columns—bases for statuary—large sundials, clocks, etc. hot-houses, aviaries—all designed as parts of architectural and landscape unit," Hearst wrote:

> Finally there are the Jersey barns, Jersey dairy and cattle fields; also the horse barn and the horse fields; a big hay barn on the hill; the kennels, etc.
>
> I have decided to keep the Jerseys on the hill as they don't have to be fed much—a dozen truckloads of hay will last them a year. One truck working a week could bring up all the hay needed for horses and Jerseys. Therefore I want to build barns for the Jerseys, the horses,

> and the hay and the pups—something like we originally planned. . . .
>
> The chickens will have to go below. They don't do well on the hill. Furthermore we will have to build the ranch dairy and some other things as agreed upon—below.
>
> What shall we do with garage hill? Shall we put the horse barn there or shall we put that down near the Jersey barn and the hay barn? Or shall we put the cow barn on the horse barn and the hay barn and dogs and everything on garage hill? Or shall we put an observatory on garage hill—with a big telescope and study the stars in our old age? Or shall we put the observatory on reservoir hill? Of course reservoir hill is the ideal spot but rather hard to get to, still it would give us another point of <u>interest</u> and a place to go to <u>see</u>.
>
> Then the water could be made a pleasant adjunct. What think? Sort of romantic isn't it! Reminds one of Washington Irving's Tales of the Alhambra, The Astrologer and the fair maiden, etc.
>
> Now we drop way down to a vegetable garden. The utilitarian takes the place of the spiritual. I think a good way to raise 'em is either in the orchards or in the little hollow at the cross roads west of Chinese hill or on a plowed plot of ground on the flats in front of Casa del Mar way down below the sequoias.
>
> I guess that's all except that there is money in wine grapes, paper shell walnuts, the finest almonds and olives and peaches and pomegranates and garlic. We ought to plant 'em.

Despite Hearst's aspirations to make "the ranch" into a paying proposition, it remained for him a showplace where he gathered his greatest pleasures and offered them for the amusement of his guests, the famous figures of the 1920s and 1930s.

A platinum print from Julia Morgan's personal papers shows the Milpitas Hacienda, a complete, if smaller, ranch complex she designed for Hearst at the northern end of the San Simeon ranch near Jolon, California. The Hacienda was built primarily to serve as an oasis for Hearst and the visitors who chose to accompany him on strenuous horseback tours of his sprawling ranch.

CHAPTER FOUR

A Glamourous &
Exciting Weekend:
Guests at San Simeon

B y the mid-1920s William Randolph Hearst's priorities were his publishing
ventures, followed by his architectural projects, art collections, and feature film
productions. Hearst's decision to move Cosmopolitan Productions, the movie-
making arm of his media empire, from New York to Hollywood in 1924 multiplied the
time he could spend at San Simeon. As Hearst's business in California increased, he
grew closer to actress Marion Davies. During their visits to San Simeon, the publisher
often worked punishing hours in his third-floor Gothic Study with Hearst Corporation
executives summoned from various publications. With the generous and openhanded
Davies came a stream of guests, invited to occupy her time on the hilltop when she
was between films.

Invitations to San Simeon, located two hundred and fifty miles north of the Hollywood studios, were the aspiration of most in the film colony. The directors, producers,
writers, and stars of the motion picture industry who received the coveted invitations
joined politicians, athletes, and other celebrities for weekends or longer stays at the
hilltop estate. Members of both W. R. and Marion's families made up the balance of
most house parties, which on weekends usually totaled about sixty people.

Guests were free to motor up the coast to San Simeon themselves. They could fly
to Hearst's private airstrip near the sea or sail up the coast when invited aboard Hearst's
yacht, the *Oneida*. Or they could join other guests at the railroad station in Los Angeles,
where the publisher's private train—complete with chef, kitchen, dining room, and club
car—awaited. Leased from Southern Pacific Railway, the train departed at seven in the

Hearst shows San Simeon guest Mrs. Burton Holmes the view from his third-floor Gothic Suite balcony, top. Teakwood carvings created by master woodcarver Jules Suppo surround them. In a 1928 snapshot, above, household staff member Joseph Reilly poses on the plane aviator-millionaire Howard Hughes had flown to San Simeon.

evening on specified days. Silent star Colleen Moore remembered a very gay trip up the coast with such frequent guests as actress-columnist Hedda Hopper, actress Constance Talmadge and her department-store-heir husband Townsend Netcher, director King Vidor and actress Eleanor Boardman, actor Adolphe Menjou and his wife Kathryn, Marion Davies' actress-friend Eileen Percy and her brewery-heir husband Eric Busch, actress Bebe Daniels and Mary Pickford's brother Jack, matinée idol John Gilbert, MGM actress Norma Shearer and her husband, producer Irving Thalberg, MGM screenwriter Carey Wilson, Hearst columnist Arthur Brisbane, and "a number of other writers from Eastern magazines, Hollywood magazines, and some of the other Hearst newspapers," Moore wrote. "There were some French diplomats and some titled English people. . . . It all added up to a very glamorous and exciting weekend for me."

Reaching San Luis Obispo in the very early hours of the morning, the Hearst train was placed on a siding. The next morning, after breakfast aboard the train, the guests were chauffeured forty-three miles up the coast by Steve Zegar's local taxi service, which Hearst had underwritten by purchasing a fleet of twelve unmarked Packards and Cadillacs in exchange for Zegar's constant availability. San Simeon staff were sometimes sent to retrieve the stray guest arriving alone.

Adela Rogers St. Johns, a writer for newspapers, magazines, and films, made her first trip to San Simeon early in her career—with Hearst himself. Planning to travel to San Simeon to see one of the Hearst magazine executives, St. Johns received a call in Los Angeles from Hearst's secretary, Joseph Willicombe:

> *"The Chief is driving up this evening and he says you may come with him if you care to." I said I cared to. . . . "Who else is going?". . . and he said, "No one." To*

most of us who worked for Mr. Hearst he came above all earthly authority and just below Jove . . . on Mount Olympus, and I was going to ride from Hollywood to San Simeon, two hundred and fifty miles, alone in an automobile with him. . . .

St. Johns overcame her awe and soon she was engaged in lively conversation with her boss about writing, college experiences, and life in California.

> *We went into a roadside diner at Los Alamos and sat on stools and Mr. Hearst said he recommended the ham and eggs or the chili so I had both. Then we got back on the road. Coming out of San Luis Obispo, where we took Coast Highway 1 by Morro Bay . . . we ran into . . . fog, . . . which thickened so the car had to cut it like a knife. We were on a one-lane . . . dirt road with no lights, no white lines, our car lights were dim. The sea was on one side, a cliff high on the other, the car twisted so Errol Flynn once got out and walked and Dolores del Rio got carsick. Our driver hung his head out [the window]. . . . Then Mr. Hearst gently said, "Here's a shoulder, pull off and I will drive."*
>
> *Thank goodness I lost my breath so I couldn't yell. . . . Here we have a trained chauffeur, it's his business, I said to myself. Mr. William Randolph Hearst owns gold mines and runs 999 newspapers and can tell presidents what to do so he thinks he can drive. . . . Fifty miles to San Simeon. Though from time to time I heard a car or the rocks bouncing down from the cliff edge, I never saw anything. Our way was as wide as the car's wheels, no wider, and as spiral as a corkscrew. We drove at a steady, fast pace, once or twice we stopped to let a gate swing open under the invisible guidance of a Mexican cowboy, we curved, climbed without a single hesitation or inch of deviation, and came to a perfect stop on the circular drive in front of what we then called*

*the Three Cottages. From that day to this
I have been sure that, whatever his faults,
Mr. Hearst could see in the dark.*

The fog had cheated St. Johns of the sight of Hearst's private zoo, the largest in the world and the result of constant planning with architect Julia Morgan. Hearst's abiding love of animals began in childhood when he was given two puppies and grew into a lifetime of affectionate regard for all animals. As the walls of his homes inspired him to collect art, the hills and meadows of his seaside estate spurred him to collect animals.

Hearst began his animal park in 1925 with herds of bison and elk kept in a Morgan-designed enclosure. In March of 1926 she wrote to Hearst, "The buffaloes have been put in the larger enclosure and looked very pretty browsing in the green grass." Fallow deer from the Mediterranean, his first imported animals, soon joined the hill-top herds. But Hearst longed for more exotic animals and retained Richard A. Addison, formerly with the San Diego Zoo, to locate and purchase animals from Africa, India, Tibet, Australia, Peru, and New Guinea.

Addison, who also located animals for director Cecil B. DeMille's Hollywood epics, was soon the recipient of typical Hearst telegrams: "CAN YOU GET PAIR ROYAL BENGAL TIGERS ALSO PLEASE GET ZEBRAS AND GIRAFFE" followed by "I WOULD LIKE ORYX" and "HAVE YOU SHIPPED BABY ELEPHANT" and "KANGAROOS HERE READY WHEN YOU COME CAR LEAVES GRAND CENTRAL STATION."

Addison usually travelled to New York or Boston, where he purchased animals directly off ships after wiring Hearst for approval. He also sometimes procured animals through famed hunter Frank (*Bring 'em Back Alive*) Buck. Addison then arranged passage for the animals on express railways across the country

to San Luis Obispo. There the animals were moved to Hearst's waiting fleet of trucks for the journey on unpaved roads to San Simeon. The giraffes presented a special problem: they were so tall that every phone and power line over Highway 1 between San Luis Obispo and San Simeon had to be taken down so the animals could pass safely. On July 27, 1927, Morgan closed a letter to Hearst:

The animals arrived in beautiful shape. I had to rub my eyes last night when out of the semi-darkness staring at the lights were grouped three ostriches, five zebras, five white deer[,] two with big horns, a llama, and some speckled deer. All in a group! The giraffes are a beautiful specimen.

An inventory of the hilltop zoo just one year later revealed more than three hundred animals, including eight kinds of antelope, five kinds of deer, forty-four bison, elk, cougars, lions, bobcats, a leopard, a cheetah, three kinds of bears, a chimpanzee, three monkeys, a tapir, sheep, goats, llamas, kangaroos, and a wallaby. A separate section of the zoo was reserved for 1,500 birds, including cassowaries, rheas, emu, macaws, parakeets, cockatoos, pigeons, swans, a pelican, a stork, pheasants, curresaws, guinea fowl, and the redundancy of two Pacific sea gulls.

Morgan was charged with housing these varied species, an unusual assignment for any architect, but doubly so when she recalled Hearst's wired wishes: "MAIN NECESSITY MUST NOT BE FORGOTTEN OF RIDING THROUGH ALL ENCLOSURES AND COMING INTO IMMEDIATE CONTACT WITH ALL ANIMALS." Morgan asked the advice of the keeper of Hamburg's Hagenbeck Zoo, a favorite of Hearst's, before designing "concrete pits for the fiercer animals, with walkways over them and enough space, pools, and caves to make the animals both comfortable and visible," according to biographer Sara Holmes Boutelle.

Zookeeper Richard Addison, top, feeds two of the field animals that thrived in Hearst's seaside meadows. Bison, elk, and deer also roamed San Simeon's hillsides in large herds. Above, actress Marion Davies poses with Marianne, the baby elephant named for her first "talkie" movie. Described as "kind of ornery" by chauffeur David Christian, Marianne was remembered by staff for trying to "squash the keeper against the side of the fence."

Dr. Barrie Carpenter, above, veterinarian for the San Simeon zoo, cuddles a tiny cub from the Hearst menagerie. Two guests, right, visit with a spotted deer on the terrace of La Casa del Sol.

A Morgan-designed house went up in 1930 for the exclusive use of Hearst's latest acquisition: an elephant. Christened "Marianne" after Marion Davies' first all-talkie movie of the same name, the baby pachyderm was a particular favorite of guests who wanted a photographic souvenir of their visit to the amazing place Hearst called home.

Various names for the private menagerie were used to get animals into the country. Addison is listed as "superintendent of the Hearst Gardens of Comparative Zoology" on a 1930 Customs form requesting importation of two giraffes and three zebras free of duty. The letterhead for the private zoo lists Addison as director of the California Garden of Comparative Zoology at San Simeon, California, with the notation "A William Randolph Hearst Activity" at the left margin.

Addison was assisted by Carey Baldwin, Hayes Perkins, and others to feed and care for Hearst's animals. Addison left San Simeon after the success of his daily newspaper feature entitled "Curious Creatures," syndicated through Hearst's King Features in New York. Addison wrote the text and drew the

panels throughout the 1930s for the feature that detailed the habits of wild and exotic animals.

Carey Baldwin, renowned among hilltop staff for his temper, was made head keeper. One memorable evening he and others worked in the keeper's shack, preparing to feed the caged animals, while the radio used to contact fellow workers on the ranch crackled with static. Without comment, Baldwin drew his sidearm, fired several rounds into the radio, replaced his gun and continued with his work.

After a few months in their new home, four giraffes were taken ill and died, which Hearst termed "a calamity." The animals had foraged from the ground, leaving many small stones in their stomachs, because the ranch was without trees tall enough for the giraffes' normal feeding habits. Troughs of suitable fodder were elevated on cranes at Hearst's direction until newly planted trees had grown high enough for the remaining giraffes to feed naturally. A few months later in January of 1932 Hearst wrote to Morgan that eleven more animals (a sable antelope, a kudu, an ibex, a sambar deer, a blackbuck, a

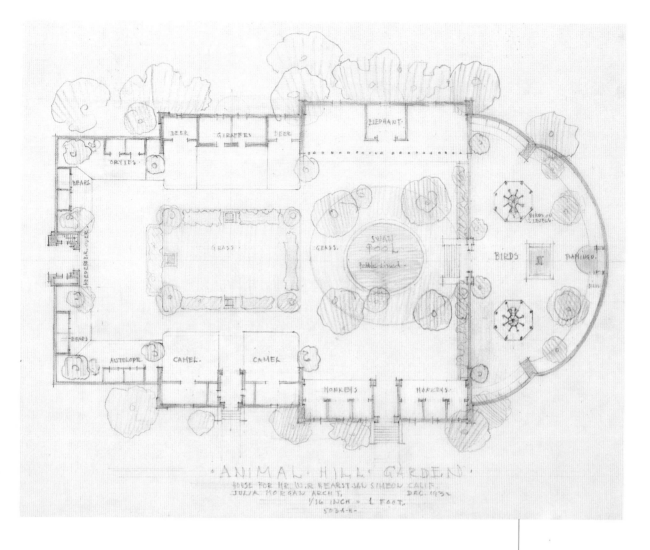

·ANIMAL·HILL·GARDEN·
HOUSE FOR MR. W.R HEARST SAN SIMEON CALIF.
JULIA MORGAN ARCH'T.   DEC. 1932
1/16 INCH = 1 FOOT.
5113-A-E-

baby oryx, a nylgau, two blesbok, and two waterbucks) had died. He wrote:

I would say they represented something like $8,000 or $10,000 in value. They were lost through exposure in heavy storms. Mr. Baldwin said that these losses occurred in spite of the best efforts of himself and staff to save these animals and [that others] would have been lost except for vigorous efforts. He said we need more shelters and some pens.

I would say that we need not only more shelters but [also] shelters that are a little more protective. I think the pens can be in connection with these shelters and I think the shelters should be more in the nature of barns than merely open shelters or protective fences. If we are going to lose $10,000 worth of animals a winter—and we may lose more than that—we can well afford to put up more shelters and

the kind which will protect the animals and keep them warm as well as dry.

Morgan made the existing shelters larger and more protective and erected three new shelters, two in the upper fields of the estate for the smaller animals and a third for larger animals. She also suggested that Hearst retain George Bistany, director of San Francisco's Fleishhacker Zoo, as a consultant. Bistany's four-page report, issued in September of 1932, was precise and candid: "The situation, in my opinion, is quite deplorable. Mr. Hearst has a collection of rare and valuable animals, and certainly they should be given proper attention to keep them healthy and in good condition." He recommended hiring additional staff for the animal park and outlined specific diets for each animal. Bistany was also

Hearst requested plans for a permanent building to house his collections of animals, urging Julia Morgan to include space for her favorite bird, the pink flamingo. The structure was never built.

BIRDS

FRONT ELEVATION.

explicit about the environment necessary
for each of the many species Hearst had
gathered together.

Hearst agreed with most of Bistany's
recommendations, wiring Morgan from
Cleveland, Ohio, at the end of October
to hire two more workers, look for a
replacement "of better temperament" for
Carey Baldwin, begin construction of
more shelters, and draw up plans for a
kitchen-hospital near the caged animals.

Hearst balked at what appeared to
be the most elemental of the directives:
segregating various animals, particularly
the buffalo, into their own enclosures. In
a lengthy letter to Morgan sent the same
day as the telegram, Hearst observed,
"What [Bistany] will have to do is find
what animals can accommodate themselves to my idea and those that cannot
do so we will get rid of." He concluded:
"I think it would be well to lay out the
hill as a park, rather than as a stiff and
ugly zoo."

But few changes were made in the
zoo's operation. Morgan drew plans for
a large animal park and central building,
but it never materialized. At its peak in
1937 Hearst's menagerie had more than
600 animals.

When actor Ralph Bellamy arrived
at San Simeon one evening for his
first visit, he was unaware that Hearst
collected animals as well as art. He
recalled, "When I came out of the
bathroom, I found my wife petrified in
the middle of the room saying, 'There's
a lion outside that window!' And I said,
'Oh, come on, it's late. We had a drink or
two. Go ahead and get your face washed
and get to bed.' When we woke up the
next morning and I went to the window,
there was a lion!" Silent-era matinée idol
Ben Lyon recalled a similar experience,
waking in the middle of the night
"scared out of my wits by a lion roaring."

Sleepless the rest of the night, actor Lyon discovered the lion and its captive companions the next morning in the cages east of the tennis courts. Though somewhat distant from the house, the caged animals howled so at night that Bellamy, Lyon, and several other guests believed them to be unnervingly close by.

Adela Rogers St. Johns was also disconcerted on her first visit, but for different reasons, as she recounted in her memoirs:

I put on a robe and rang, and asked the maid who came—there was twenty-four-hour service of all kinds—for coffee. With a pleasant smile she said I would have to go up to the Castle for that. This was almost the only thing I found difficult about the ranch. All the years I went there, sometimes I spent weeks at a time, I had to get dressed, walk paths between white statues and flowering trees to the Castle for my coffee; or after the big main building was finished and I was usually in the Doge's Suite on the second floor, dress and walk down flights of stone or tiled or marble stairs. At home I had coffee the moment I opened my eyes. I once asked Marion Davies about this incongruous bit amid the luxury, the meticulous service, and extravagant indulgence by which guests were surrounded. She said W. R. did not approve of breakfast in bed. If people did not get up and get dressed they might frowst away hours that could better be spent outdoors. He thought, Marion said, that the wonderful walk through morning dew and freshness with the sparkle of the sea below . . . was a good way to start the day. I'm sure it was but at the time I thought I could have appreciated it more with one cup of coffee under my riding britches or my tennis skirt.

Those guests who traveled by train and limousine to San Simeon usually arrived in the late morning. Once on the hilltop, the chauffeurs drove around the estate's U-shaped road to Joseph Willicombe's office. Guests were greeted at the southern flight of stairs off the main terrace by the housekeeper, who welcomed them on behalf of Hearst and Davies, located their rooms, and urged them to ring for a member of the staff for

Actress Marion Davies poses for a fashion layout on the terrace at San Simeon, left.

Traveler-bibliophile A. Edward Newton visited San Simeon with famed San Francisco printer John Henry Nash in the early 1930s. In his memoirs, Newton recalled:

> . . . After motoring for several hours [Nash] said to me, "We are now on Mr. Hearst's ranch." We had entered no gates and there was nothing to suggest that we were on a private estate; we were just speeding along a country road. "That is the port of San Simeon . . . ," said my friend. "When Mr. Hearst sees anything he wants, he buys it and sends it here. If it fits into his scheme, he uses it; if it doesn't, he puts it in storage. Those are his warehouses." Presently we came to a wooden gate, one of those "grasshopper" gates which leap sideways into the air by the pulling of a rope. I did the pulling, taking the opportunity to read a sign on the gate, "Beware of animals." I didn't see any, but, knowing where I was, I promptly bewared and . . . hurried into the motor. After a mile or two we came to another gate, this time guarded by a man who came out from a small cabin. "Are you expected?" he said. "What name?" I saw wires leading from the cabin, and no doubt our names were telephoned to the mansion. Permission to enter was soon accorded.

Butler Albert Redelsperger watches over Hearst and his luncheon guests in the Refectory, right. Guest A. E. Newman wrote, "Mr. Hearst's menu promised little and performed much. It was an ample, delicious, but not elaborate luncheon, beautifully served. . . . [Hearst] drank two small glasses of excellent claret; wine and spirits were to be had, but the guests, like the host, drank very little." The "excellent claret" Newton enjoyed came from Hearst's extensive wine cellar, above, housed in a basement vault in the main building.

the smallest necessity. For unprepared guests, an array of toiletries as well as bathing suits, trunks, caps, riding clothes, and boots in various sizes were available. Houseboys took their luggage and escorted guests to their rooms, where a card listed the day's menu and hours for meals, as well as the title of the evening film.

Sam Shupper, an electrician from North Hollywood, worked for three weeks at San Simeon in 1928, installing a sound system that was quite sophisticated at the time. In most of the main building's guest bedrooms, Shupper wired in speakers and a control panel that allowed guests to listen to a daily selection of records played on a phono-graph in a vault in the basement. Guests could also use the controller to tune in six radio stations from San Francisco and Los Angeles. The system was designed so that there was no need for a radio or phonograph in each room. According to Shupper, the music "played through a speaker system in the rooms. . . . Some person would go down there in the basement every day and change the stack of records in the Capehart player and then he would bring a list into each room."

After guests were acquainted with the amenities in their rooms, they gathered between 1 and 2 PM on the terrace in front of the main building, where Hearst and Davies customarily made their first appearance. Luncheon

was a simple but leisurely meal, often served buffet-style in La Casa Grande's huge dining hall, the Refectory, where members of the house party were introduced to each other and made plans for the day. Afternoons were free for swimming, horseback riding, tennis, or a visit to the zoo and kennels. Picnics on the beach or extended trips on horseback about the ranch were also possibilities.

Edward Newton, who stayed in the second-floor Doge's Suite, recalled that soon after his arrival "someone knocked on my door and asked if I wanted to ride, motor, shoot, golf, swim, or play tennis, and he seemed very much surprised when I said, 'Not if I can help it.' He bowed, as who should say, 'This is liberty hall,' and presently I began to wander over the mansion, castle, palace—call it by what name you will; they all apply—seeking what I knew I should find—the library."

When indoor pursuits were necessary, games of billiards, poker, and bridge were undertaken and a large chest at the north end of the Assembly Room yielded jigsaw puzzles and board games, including Chinese checkers, dominoes, bingo, and Monopoly. An informal lending library of current bestsellers and popular literature was available in secretary Joseph Willicombe's office. By ten each morning, copies of the Los Angeles *Examiner*, other Hearst newspapers, and Hollywood trade papers such

As guest A. E. Newton entered San Simeon's Refectory, above, for the first time, he "had the feeling we were about to regale ourselves in one of the lesser halls of Windsor Castle." Of his first time waiting table in the Refectory, Fred Redelsperger recalled, "I know that when I went into the dining room, it was a brand-new experience. It scared the hell out of me . . ."

The scene of many lively parties, the Assembly Room, above, had a disguised door to the left of the fireplace through which Hearst would enter the room. The Assembly Room, which illustrator Ludwig Bemelmans described as "half of Grand Central Station," covers nearly 2,500 square feet.

The Morning Room, opposite, or Breakfast Room, as it was called in Hearst's day, is decorated for Christmas with masses of greens and poinsettias.

Hearst was not zealous about making visitors commemorate their stays in a guest book, bottom right, but several examples, including this one from spring of 1929, were found among the estate's papers.

as *The Hollywood Reporter* and *Variety*, were available on the vast center table of the Assembly Room.

Ella "Bill" Williams, Davies' secretary, often coached first-time guests, who were understandably nervous given the power of their host and grandeur of their surroundings, about Hearst's preferences and the unwritten rules. Although guests were permitted to bring liquor, they were not to drink to excess.

Actor David Niven, a frequent guest, would later recall that "wine flowed like glue during [dinner], and afterward it might just be possible to extract an occasional glass of California champagne from the butler, but [Hearst's] eye would be on everyone's intake, particularly that of Marion." Those who over-imbibed returned to their rooms to find their bags already packed and a car waiting nearby to dispatch them with celerity off the

hill. Actor Errol Flynn and author Dorothy Parker were but two visitors who were, in euphemistic terms, "sent down the hill."

Of her visits to San Simeon, socialite Gloria Vanderbilt, Sr., wrote in her memoirs:

Life in this Hearstian empire is lived according to the disciplinary measures laid down by its dictator. No one is permitted to bring one's own personal maid—a maid or valet is assigned to you immediately on your arrival. You are permitted to do as you like in the mornings; there are only two things asked of guests at San Simeon—that you appear promptly in what is called the Great Hall each evening . . . to await your host. . . . It is an understood thing that no drinks are ever served until just before dinner hours, and then only in the Great Hall.

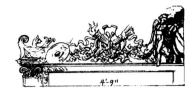

Hilding "Pete" Kruslock, a carpenter at San Simeon, remembered a special job:

Money was no object. What the old man wanted, he got. I remember when the jigsaw puzzles first came out—that was years ago—one of his guests was putting it together, and there was one little piece missing. And, of course, they had to have a carpenter come and make a little piece that fit in that little hole, just about the size of a quarter or four-bit piece. I was the one elected. I had to get a little piece of wood and cut it to the thickness of that cardboard and try to make it fit in that place. And, of course, you know, I felt like I was all thumbs and no fingers in doing it. Eventually got it to fit. And then they sent for the head decorator [artist Camille Solon] to go in there and finish the design. [Afterwards], nine chances out of ten, it was shoved in the wastepaper basket and that was the end of it.

Painter-author Ludwig Bemelmans came to Hollywood in 1943 when a story he co-wrote was adapted for the 1945 Fred Astaire film *Yolanda and the Thief*. He visited San Simeon at the urging of his friend, interior decorator-socialite Elsie Lady Mendl, who praised Hearst's art collections and their San Simeon setting. After Hearst's death Bemelmans published an acidulous account of his stay and his host. Of the "Great Hall," or Assembly Room, whose size he estimated as "half of Grand Central Station," Bemelmans wrote:

Looking with the eyes of Elsie, I wondered about her genie, Good Taste, and the three attendants, Simplicity, Suitability, and Proportion. Couches all over, and in one corner, hiding in the lower half of the marble woman [statue], a radio cabinet done to match the room— a bad Gothic imitation of such woodcutting as the . . . altars in southern Bavaria, with figures in a very foreshortened perspective. . . and dark stuff smeared into the deep parts to make it antique.

In the center of the room was a fireplace that reached the sixty-foot ceiling, and this by contrast was superbly beautiful—perhaps the rarest fireplace in the world—of great tenderness, magnificent color a breathless living monument, a perfect thing, big as the façade of a house. A few feet away stood a dreadful rosewood piano with a carmine coverlet of the unhappiest texture and shade.

Adorned in a fashionable frock and picture hat, Marion Davies, above, poses for an MGM still photographer on a San Simeon terrace.

W. R. Hearst's second son, William Randolph, Jr., and his wife Lorelle sunbathe on the terrace surrounding the Neptune Pool, right.

The terrace, opposite, located south of the main terrace, features two marble wellheads. Gardener Norman Rotanzi recalled this site as the gathering place in the late afternoon for household staff to relax before beginning their evening duties.

Most visitors found the pre-dinner cocktail party in the Assembly Room a lively affair, as guests in glamorous attire conversed animatedly or played Mah-jongg as cocktails were dispensed from a large silver tray at the south end of the room. The entire time a gramophone thumped out the latest popular tunes: "I'm in the Mood for Love," "Flying Down to Rio," "She Had to Go and Lose It at the Astor," "A Peach of a Pair," "The Very Thought of You," "Shakin' the Blues Away," "If I Could Be with You One Hour Tonight," and "I Only Have Eyes for You."

Hearst and Davies entered from a door in the east wall that was disguised by the monastery choir stalls bordering the room. The house party was usually alerted to their arrival by the presence of Hearst and Davies' dachshunds, Helen and Ghandi. After newcomers were presented to Hearst (they usually knew Davies), the entire group moved next door to the great dining hall. Placecards indicated the seating along the four highly polished walnut refectory tables, made in Italy in the seventeenth century, which were placed end to end in the center of the room.

David Niven recalled: "Hearst sat in the middle of the table. Marion sat directly opposite him, and I noticed that his cold blue eyes . . . were looking warmly at her throughout the meal. In the middle section of the table, flanking W. R. and herself, Marion had parked the elder statesmen and stateswomen of the group, while the boys [Hearst's sons], their wives, and their friends, jogging the arms of the wine-serving Filipino servants in vain attempts to encourage respectable rations, were phased out into the half-light at either end."

Augusta Redelsperger was Hearst's housekeeper; her husband, Albert, served as butler in the mid-1930s. The Redelspergers' son, Fred, recalled the vast scope of his parents' responsibilities overseeing the household staff. As butler, Albert "didn't . . . just run around and serve drinks," remembered Fred. "He planned all the food, bought all the food, saw that it was cooked properly, saw that it was served properly, and the right decor as far as the dining room was concerned, for the guests and Mr. Hearst." After planning the week's menus with the chef, Redelsperger sought

Fred Redelsperger, who worked for his father, Hearst's butler Albert Redelsperger, as a waiter during Christmas and vacations, recalled the visit of famed British playwright and curmudgeon George Bernard Shaw in 1933:

> I almost had an accident with him. We were serving plum pudding . . . you pour brandy over it and you light it. . . . I had graduated from being a dishwasher to becoming a waiter. I was relatively inexperienced, but I had the stance . . . and I knew how to say, "Excuse me," and so on. And as I said, "Excuse me, Mr. Shaw," and he turned around [suddenly], I had that plum pudding burning there. Of course with the blue flames, you don't see it. And he turned around and almost lit his beard. I backed off and he backed off, and he said, "You saved my beard!"

Hearst's approval and then wrote each dinner's courses in an elegant, flowing script on parchment for the table.

Waiters from the Ambassador Hotel in Los Angeles were recruited to train local staff in the art of waiting table. For large house parties, according to Redelsperger, five waiters from the Ambassador Hotel were imported to augment the three permanent members of the dining room staff. Of his stint as a waiter under his father's tutelage, Redelsperger recalled, "[My] duties started probably at eight in the morning and sometimes they lasted until twelve at night. . . . I know that when I went into the dining room, it was a brand-new experience. It scared the hell out of me."

In 1939 Norman Francis, whose father was keeper of the nearby Piedras Blancas lighthouse, worked "extra" on the household staff when large house parties were in residence. Francis recollected that Hearst employees were envied locally as much as his father was for his secure civil service job. When called for work at the estate, Francis arrived "early! Then you'd simply spend the day [as assigned]. Most of my day was spent in the kitchen," with periodic trips to "load

In a 1930s snapshot, Prince Louis Ferdinand Hohenzollern of Liechtenstein poses with head housekeeper Augusta Redelsperger and household staff member Lee Wenzlik.

up fireplaces for the evening. . . .Everyone loved to work up there because you cleared a couple of dollars a day and you picked up two or three pounds." Throughout the 1930s, Hearst paid three dollars per day for temporary help, with a dollar held back for meals, a plan similar to that for construction workers.

Fred Redelsperger remembered, "Waiters used to nibble a little bit on the things that were left on the platters [and the food] was gourmet, all right. Best beef in the world. . . . They had some pretty exotic food." Tablecloths were not used because Hearst preferred seeing the highly polished walnut of the antique tables, but linen napkins were used "that'd blow ninety-nine percent of the budget. Everything was first class, it really was."

Maurice McClure was one of very few individuals who made the transition from construction laborer to a member of the household staff. Of his household job, McClure remembers, "I fed the fireplaces, carried suitcases, did a little bit of local chauffeuring, and that kind of work." The firewood was bought from local ranchers and farmers because Hearst "did not want a tree [on his property] cut down and burned" to feed the estate's forty-one fireplaces. McClure later became San Simeon's fourth and final construction superintendent.

Mel Engle, who was hired as a waiter in 1939, recalled what it was like to work for the publisher:

> *Mr. Hearst was extremely knowledgeable as to the property that he had, particularly the glassware and dishes. One time, I accidentally broke the stem off of a rose-colored cut crystal goblet, so it couldn't be put back in the cabinet. There was obviously a blank space there. Well, I happened to know that down in the cellar, underneath the kitchen area, was a storage area down there. There was a supply of these same goblets down there, so I got one and replaced the [broken] one with the one that wasn't.*

> *Within the same week, Mr. Hearst was through and wondered what happened to the goblet that was missing. He . . . knew that much about his things.*

Hearst's capacity for detail amazed everyone except, perhaps, Julia Morgan and Joseph Willicombe. Electrician Byron Hanchett recalls Hearst even noticed at one point that the weather vanes atop the main building's towers were blowing in different directions, a problem that was soon remedied.

Engle recalled spending workdays "dusting, squeezing oranges, then be[ing] ready to serve dinner by 7:00 in the evening, but we might not serve until midnight. . . .There was always the cleanup period, and we'd get that taken care of while the guests were milling around after dinner. By the time we got cleaned up, they were usually moving on into the theater. As soon as they turned the theater lights out, we'd all duck into the theater and watch the show. . . . After the theater time, they would usually wander back again, socialize a bit, have a few drinks, then Mr. Hearst would leave the group . . . [for] his editorial work from say 12 or 1 o'clock, until say five or six in the morning."

Although a printed schedule was distributed, meal times on the hilltop were set only when Hearst would descend from the Gothic Library. Butler Albert Redelsperger often had to placate the chefs when meals were delayed. Fred Redelsperger recalled looking back at the main building as he left at 2 AM and seeing lights in Hearst's third-floor study. Hearst "worked pretty near all night. He stayed with his newspapers so they'd come out early in the morning. And he would work all night long. He'd go to bed about four or five o'clock. And then he wouldn't get up until about one or two o'clock and that first meal of the day was his brunch, or lunch and

breakfast, at two o'clock in the afternoon, buffet style. Then the next meal would be ten o'clock at night. And then after that, movie time."

At San Simeon "movie time" meant the screening of a newsreel, followed by a feature-length motion picture, not yet available to the public and supplied by Hollywood studios "hoping to garner some favorable publicity by this genuflection in the direction of the all-important Hearst press," wrote actor David Niven. Architect Julia Morgan gave a great deal of time and attention to Hearst's private theater, knowing her client's fondness for the medium and its importance to the social life of San Simeon. Fifteen-foot-high gilded caryatids, or draped female figures, provided support for the walls, electric light, and decorative interest. Morgan custom-ordered the fifty overstuffed loge seats done in red brocade and

gold velvet that fill the 90 x 30 foot room. The screen recessed into the floor so the small stage could be used for impromptu live entertainment by Hearst's talented guests.

Hearst and Davies sat in the front row; next to Hearst was a telephone with a direct line to the projection booth and buttons that enabled him to raise or lower the sound. Morgan also added a metal barrier between the projection booth and the audience in the event of fire caused by the combustible nitrate stock used for movies in the 1920s and 1930s. Morgan provided a separate generator to power the projectors because the electrical current often fluctuated at the remote location.

When a large group of guests was present on the hill, Hearst ordered two shows, one for employees in the early evening and a late screening following dinner for guests and the kitchen help.

The lower lobby of La Casa del Mar features an Italian polychrome statue of the Virgin and a traditional plaster bas-relief from the sixteenth century.

Dalmacio Carpio, a San Simeon chef, remembered seeing "movies [before] they'd been released from the studio. . . . Sometimes when they got a good picture and Miss Davies came to the kitchen, 'Dally, tell all the boys, all the help, to come and see the picture. It's good.' 'Are you sure it's good?' 'I promise, it's good.' "

After attending many of the late night screenings with the elite of Hollywood in Hearst's private theater, actor David Niven reflected, "To an unknown actor it was a revelation and a mixed joy to listen to the acid comments and catcalls that greeted some of the efforts that were selected nightly for dissection. It was a rough audience for a bad film, but the best audience in the world for a good one."

Social life at San Simeon thrived amid the constant din of construction, but by 1937 Hearst's personal and business finances were precarious. Hearst's unrestrained buying and building sprees had aggravated his financial woes. It was estimated that

there were at least ninety companies under the Hearst Corporation name; each had borrowed from banks and other Hearst companies until the indebtedness was estimated at $126 million.

In June of 1937 Hearst signed over his controlling stock in the primary holding corporation to Judge Clarence J. Shearn, a friend and lawyer. Hearst retained control of editorial policy, but his finances were now in other hands for the first time since his mother had bestowed the proceeds from the Anaconda mines on him almost forty-five years earlier.

It was less easy to persuade Hearst to part with his vast treasure trove of antiquities or his magnificent estates. Advisers recommended that at least two-thirds of the art must be sold to avoid inheritance taxes and to provide a cash infusion to the corporation. The fifth floor of Gimbel Brothers department store was transformed, according to the *Saturday Evening Post*, into a "gigantic bazaar of the arts." Thousands of art objects, including paneling, ceilings, stained glass, paintings, and

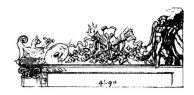

sculpture, covered 100,000 square feet of
space in the store. The initial two-month
period, during which Gimbels assumed
the role of agent and received a commission on each piece sold, was so successful
it was extended for fourteen months. *The
New York Times* noted, "Armor, of which
Hearst had enough to stage a successful
siege of his castle of St. Donat, sold from
$4.50 up. Egyptian statuettes, tagged at
35, 60 and 95 cents, were among the
fifteen thousand items. . . . "

The English silver, including
pieces from the Tudor, Stuart, and early
Georgian periods, were sold at Sotheby's
London office. Books and manuscripts

were auctioned at Parke-
Bernet Galleries
in New York
City; items that
did not meet the
minimum bids were
sent to Gimbels to
be put on sale. The
animals in Hearst's
private collection were
donated to zoos around
the country, with the
exception of field animals
that required minimal
attention. Zebras and
goats from the original

San Simeon guests who strolled along the esplanade in spring encountered azaleas in profuse bloom, above. Fortune magazine described the Hearst estate's main building, opposite, in 1931: "In the fabulous Casa Grande which crowns [the estate] . . . are chefs-d'ouevre from the collection of the great collector of objets d'art in the world."

zoo still roam the ranchland that surrounds the estate.

His financial position improved greatly when the government purchased a large tract of land from Hearst's San Simeon acreage for Fort Hunter-Liggett, an army installation. The advent of World War II meant a sharp increase in newspaper sales, which further strengthened the publisher's finances. During the war, Hearst and Davies spent a great deal of time at Wyntoon because it was believed that San Simeon was vulnerable to Japanese attack. As World War II drew to a close, they returned to San Simeon, where construction resumed on the north wing of the main building under the direction of Warren McClure, Morgan's protégé. Morgan and Hearst also began plans for a hacienda at his million-acre ranch in Chihuahua, Mexico.

In 1947 a heart attack forced him to leave the hilltop; he and Davies retreated to a relatively modest Beverly Hills estate at 1007 Lexington Drive to be close to the specialists who attempted to maintain his faltering health. The finest fruits, vegetables, and poultry San Simeon produced were sent to him in Beverly Hills.

Although he longed to return to "the ranch," Hearst was never to see it again. On August 14, 1951, William Randolph Hearst died at the age of eighty-eight from the combined effects of a stroke and "ailments of advanced age."

San Simeon today is a lasting and unique tribute to the collaboration of architect Julia Morgan and her best-known client, William Randolph Hearst. Perhaps waiter Mel Engle summed it up best: "At night, with all the lights on around the terrace, music coming from inside the Castle, moonlight shimmering down on San Simeon Bay, it was like paradise up here."

Bibliography

Armstrong, Jane. "Woman Architect Who Helped Build the Fairmont Hotel." *Architect and Engineer of California* (October 1907): 69-71.

Bemelmans, Ludwig. *To the One I Love the Best.* New York: Viking Press, 1955.

Boutelle, Sara Holmes. *Julia Morgan, Architect.* New York: Abbeville Press, 1988.

Burgess, R.L. "Working for Hearst." *The New Republic* 71.923 (10 August 1932): 340-342.

Denning, Roy, et. al. *The Story of St. Donat's Castle and Atlantic College.* Cowbridge: D. Brown and Sons, 1983.

Fredericksen, Burton. *Handbook of Paintings in the Hearst San Simeon State Historical Monument.* [S.l.]: Delphinian Publications, 1976.

Hanchett, Byron. *In and Around the Castle.* San Luis Obispo, California: Blake Printery, 1985.

"Hearst." *Fortune* 12.4 (October 1935): 42-55+.

"Hearst at Home." *Fortune* 3.5 (May 1931): 56-58, 130.

Hearst San Simeon State Historical Monument Oral History Project interviews: Ralph Bellamy (1981); Zel and Leon Bordegary (1988); Dalmacio Carpio (1981); David Christian (1983); Bjarne Dahl, Jr. (1983); Mel Engle (1988); Sherman Eubanks (1984); Norman Francis (1990); Charles Gates (1978); Joseph Giarritta (1988); Stanley Heaton and Elmer Moorhouse (1984); Fred Jordan (1979); Hilding "Pete" Kruslock (1973); Brayton Laird (1986); George Loorz (1975); Maurice McClure (1981); Ann Miller (1977); Guido Minetti (1982); John Pellegrini (1973); Fred Redelsperger (1985); Milton and Eileen Rohrberg (1977); Norman Rotanzi (1977 and 1988); Sam Shupper (1981); Franklin and Helen Whitcomb (1983).

Hearst, William Randolph, Jr. with Jack Casserly. *The Hearsts: Father and Son.* Niwot, Colorado: Roberts Rinehart, 1991.

"The Julia Morgan Architectural History Project," ed. Suzanne Reiss. Berkeley, California: The Bancroft Library, Regional Oral History Office, University of California, 1976.

Julia Morgan Collection, Special Collections Department, Kennedy Library, California Polytechnic State University, San Luis Obispo.

Loe, Nancy E. *Hearst Castle: The Official Pictorial Guide.* Santa Barbara: ARA Leisure Services, Inc., 1991.

—. *William Randolph Hearst: An Illustrated Biography.* Santa Barbara: ARA Leisure Services, Inc., 1988.

Moore, Colleen. *Silent Star.* Garden City, New York: Doubleday, 1968.

Newton, A. Edward. *Derby Day and Other Adventures.* Boston: Little, Brown, 1934.

Pavlik, Robert C. " 'Something A Little Different': La Cuesta Encantada's Architectural Precedents and Cultural Prototypes." 71.4 *California History* (Winter 1992/93): 462-477.

Perkins, Hayes. "Here and There: The Diary of Hayes Perkins." Unpublished manuscript, 1928-1936. Courtesy of Mrs. Jane E. Preston.

Phoebe Apperson Hearst Papers 72/204c, The Bancroft Library, University of California, Berkeley.

"Reference and Study Manual: Guide Section." San Simeon, California: Hearst San Simeon State Historical Monument, 1990.

"Register mit doorslagen van ultgaande brieven van Klokkengierterij Michiels te Doornik, 1921." Gemeentelijke Archiefdienst Helmond, Archief Petit & Fritsen, inventarisnummer 282.

St. Johns, Adela Rogers. *The Honeycomb.* Garden City, New York: Doubleday, 1969.

Scharlath, Bernice. "The Legacy of Julia Morgan." *California Living Magazine: The Sunday* [San Francisco] *Examiner and Chronicle* (24 August 1975): 24.

Vanderbilt, Gloria Morgan with Palma Wayne. *Without Prejudice.* New York: E.P. Dutton, 1936.

Wadsworth, Virginia. *Julia Morgan: Architect of Dreams.* Minneapolis: Lerner, 1990.